Codename: Scarlett

★ ★ ★

*Life on the Campaign Trail
by the Wife of a
Presidential Candidate*

Codename:
SCARLETT

★ ★ ★

*Life on the Campaign Trail
by the Wife of a
Presidential Candidate*

JEANNE SIMON

CONTINUUM | NEW YORK

1989

The Continuum Publishing Company
370 Lexington Avenue
New York, NY 10017

Printed in the United States of America

Library of Congress Cataloging-in-Publication Data

Simon, Jeanne.
    Codename Scarlett : life on the campaign trail / by the wife of a
presidential candidate, Jeanne Simon.
        p.   cm.
    ISBN 0-8264-0437-5
    1. Presidents—United States—Election—1988.   2. Simon, Paul,
1928–   .   3. Simon, Jeanne.   4. Presidential candidates—United
States—Biography.   5. Politicians' wives—United States—Biography.
I. Title.
E880.S64   1989
973.927′092′2—dc19
    [B]   88-35967
                                                                    CIP

To Martin, Sheila, and Perry

Contents

Introduction

There have been many books about presidential candidates and their campaigns, mostly in the genre of Theodore White's *The Making of a President*. There will be many books written about the presidential campaign of 1988. I have been interviewed at length by four of these authors, and I know there are others. One author is my husband, Senator Paul Simon. Anyone who follows a campaign of one candidate closely for a period of time develops a keen interest in the fate of that candidate. His or her insights and perceptions of events that make or break a campaign are valuable. But my story is different.

I have had an interest in politics all my life—Democratic politics. Born in Chicago, I grew up on the North Shore with a strong Irish-Catholic, Democratic family in the era of Mayor Daley and FDR. My father, Ira W. Hurley, a lawyer active in local Democratic circles, predicted before his death in early 1951 that Adlai Stevenson would be the Democratic candidate for president in 1952. How I wish that he could have celebrated with my two brothers and mother my victory in 1956: election to the Illinois General Assembly as State Representative for the Seventh District. And how I wish he could have met State Representative Paul Simon from Madison County, the man I married in 1960.

Paul and I and our two children, Sheila and Martin, share a love of public service and make it an integral part of our lives. When Paul made his first statewide race for lieutenant governor in 1968, our kids—then seven and four—wore sweatshirts that said "Vote for my Daddy." We made every election a family effort and enjoyed each one. All these primaries and elections (that included one major loss) climaxed in the year of our lives that started April 9, 1987, and ended April 7, 1988.

This campaign differed from all the rest, but we were ready for it in many ways, once we made the decision to enter the race. When we made that decision, I realized this would be a unique experience for all of us and that I would keep a journal of the campaign as I saw it. I thought it would be great fun to read in years to come, just for our family. It doesn't happen to every family in the United States, and there is a very small group of women who have been privileged to take part in this process with their husbands. As one of this group, with a good background in politics, I could judge persons and events with a sense of history. But my journal is not about making policy or the nuts and bolts of organization charts or about the endless chore of fund-raising, although I had something to do with all these.

My journal and book is the view of a candidate's wife, a person between the candidate and staff, who took an active part in the campaign, most of the time on my own, not accompanying Paul. The candidate works hard. I know that. He is also the candidate, with all the perks of being the candidate. The "wife of," as they usually referred to me in introductions, sees and does things with a lot less glamour and attention. Early on, I learned that a sense of humor is essential. Coping with schedules that were really jammed, the problems of laundry and dry cleaning (I frequently had dry cleaning in three states), trying to remember the names of all the people along the way and, most of all, trying to look like and sound like a believable occupant of the White House—all of this called for a supreme effort. But it was fun.

Not long ago, the wives of presidential candidates traveled with their mates all the time and confined their campaign activities to wearing a large white orchid and responding to the inevitable introduction, ". . . and in back of every successful man, there is a helpful wife. . ." with a smile and a wave. Their passive role or decorative one gave the candidate an opportunity to show himself as a fine family man. With the increasing number of women office holders, professional and working women, the advocacy role of many women's groups, and the candidacy of Geraldine Ferraro on the Democratic ticket in 1984, the electorate not only wanted to see the candidates' wives but to hear them as well. We owe a debt of gratitude to Geraldine Ferraro and Walter Mondale for that.

The indiscretions of Senator Gary Hart, which came to light shortly after Paul's campaign began, created additional curiosity about "the wives" on the part of the press and public. Lee Hart ran the gauntlet of a merciless press, and for some time after Senator Hart's withdrawal on May 8, 1987, the first question any reporter asked would be my reaction to the whole affair.

I wanted to talk about *Paul,* what he had accomplished in Congress and what his hopes were for the future of our country. And I did—in Iowa and New Hampshire, Minnesota, South Dakota, Illinois, Wisconsin, and many other states. I didn't always make a nice little, general speech, meet and mingle (M&M was our abbreviation for that), and leave. Usually we allowed an opportunity for questions from the audience, not all of whom thought Paul the right choice.

When a row of students at St. Cloud State University in Minnesota all sported big Dole buttons, I knew I would have some tough questions. When a super smart high school student in Nashua, New Hampshire, wanted to engage in a dialogue on some esoteric topic, I tried to remain calm and give a rather general answer and hoped that another student would ask a question I could answer. I was expected to have all the answers that Paul had at his command, based on his years of congressional service and the immediate and thorough help from his staff. This frequently caused me to make emergency calls to our campaign office for facts and figures, voting records, and reactions to current events. When the press asked a question, I wanted to give a sound answer, and that took study of the issues in detail. Gradually I developed my own stump speech and a few lines that I knew would be well received by a Democratic audience. Congressman Dave Nagle of Iowa spoke about Paul and President Reagan in a speech, saying, "Paul has written eleven books, which is probably ten more than Ronald Reagan has read." Without attribution, I used that line many times.

Speaking to a group of any size was never easy, and the presence of a TV camera only served to exacerbate the situation. I hated to see myself on TV, and I never felt completely comfortable trying to sound confident while hoping I was looking at the right camera and not talking too fast. Appearing on the CBS "Morning Show," "Good Morning America," and the NBC "Today" show were great experiences now that I can look back, but not at the time. My first national TV appearance was a momentous event, and only with coaching in TV skills from my good friend and staff person, Lea Sinclair, was I able to feel at all confident.

Whatever the situation, I realized that I represented Paul and worked hard to make my audience appreciate his ability as I did. I also realized (because frequently people would tell me) that they judged me on my ability to contribute to Paul's administration, and I loved it when some kind person would say, "Well, I don't know if I'll vote for Paul, but I'd sure vote for you!"

Trying to be the best candidate's wife possible and to be without Paul on the campaign trail most of the time; to keep his morale high when mine was low; to cope with all the exigencies that included lost luggage (Northwest Airlines promptly sent me a check for my loss), a serious car accident (but I made it to the next meeting with the help of the sheriff), hasty meals en route or sometimes no meals at all (I began to appreciate candy bars again), or working out the details of our daughter's wedding in September—all these things and many more were part of the campaign. I look back on the notes in my journal and wonder how all of us managed to get through twelve months of uncertainty with last-minute changes in schedules, illnesses of our children (Martin had the flu for two days, alone in a motel), the ups and downs of the polls, the cartoons that I didn't always think were amusing, stories that distorted Paul's statements, and the ubiquitous debates, each one with its own set of rigid rules and procedures.

Campaigning with Secret Service agents round the clock was something new for a Simon campaign. Initially, Paul and I thought their presence would hamper his access to people; but Agents Tim Scanlon, Lee Waggoner, Bob Turner, and John Parker, who were in charge of Paul's detail (code name "Scarlett"), adapted their protective measures to his style of campaigning. People were curious about the Secret Service. One woman wanted to know if I had to feed them when they were at our home in Makanda or at our apartment in Washington. (I didn't!)

I won't forget the young student couple and their baby who gave up their "fun money" for three months to join a special fund-raiser event; the campaign staff in New Hampshire who waited in the bitter cold on a hillside to greet us with banners and cheers; the charming "bed and breakfast" home where I stayed with Jim and Evelyn Hodges in Burlington, Iowa. Nor will I forget the thrill of learning about the endorsement of the *Des Moines Register* on January 31, 1988; going from a size 12 to a size 10 dress without even trying; the bliss of wearing old jeans on a rare day off; the pleasure of brief reunions with Sheila and Martin; the joy of being with Paul from time to time.

When it ended on the morning of April 7, 1988, there were no tears. A week in Puerto Rico for all of us helped the adjustment back to normalcy. But life will never be quite the same for me. I was part of an almost unique American experience—and made a contribution to the democratic process.

That experience is what this book is about. And there are no ghost writers for this author. It is my story; these are my words.

★ 1 ★

The Big Decision—
April 9, 1987

First Journal Entry—
At 10:30 A.M. today Paul walked into the Mike
Mansfield Room of the U.S. Senate and announced
that he is a candidate for President of the United States.
April 9, 1987

Our son Martin and I, with pride and misty eyes, watched Paul make his short and dramatic declaration of candidacy that included a ringing phrase to be heard many, many times in the coming months, "I am not a neo-anything, I am a Democrat."

The official opening of the campaign would follow—May 18, 1987—in Carbondale, Illinois, the home of Southern Illinois University, near our home in rural Makanda. The room in Washington was jammed with friends, supporters, Senate staffers; and Paul faced a galaxy of microphones, TV cameras, and reporters. The last time we had seen such a press turnout was the day after Paul won his Senate seat, November 7, 1984, when our daughter Sheila, Martin, and I stood in the back of a crowded room in the Ambassador West Hotel in Chicago and cheered lustily for the victory of the "underdog" in the Reagan landslide that washed over Illinois.

Two incumbent Republican senators were defeated in that election: Senators Jepsen and Percy. Roger Jepsen of Iowa, a one-term senator, who chanced to use his American Express credit card in a massage parlor in Iowa, seemed doomed to defeat by Congressman Tom Harkin almost from the start, according to the polls and public opinion. Senator Charles Percy of Illinois was an eighteen-year veteran. As chairman of the Senate Foreign Relations Committee, he had a substantial campaign treasury and a lot of help from the Reagan administration folks, including many joint appearances with Reagan in Illinois. His victory seemed assured, with strong endorsements from the Chicago newspapers and an impressive lead in all the polls.

Paul's narrow victory, 90,000 votes out of 4.5 million cast, was the outstanding Democratic victory of an otherwise gloomy year for Democrats. Favorable press attention followed the election, including a piece by syndicated columnist Richard Reeves and an article by Michael Kilian in the *Chicago Tribune* magazine, hinting that Paul would be a strong candidate for the Democratic nomination for president in 1988. Several of Paul's House colleagues sent him a letter urging him to consider becoming a candidate. I loved all this recognition of Paul's ability but did not give it serious consideration. Indeed, I looked forward to a six-year term with a great deal of joy.

Ever since we were married (April 21, 1960, after the Illinois primary), we had been involved in an election every two years, with a few exceptions. We met in the Illinois General Assembly as state representatives. Paul was from downstate while I represented five large suburbs of Chicago. My brief career as a state representative (two terms) ended when I moved to Troy following our marriage, but I maintained a keen interest in elections and politics. While I missed the give and take as a participant in the legislative process, I continued to campaign with and for Paul, and kept up with current issues. The challenge of an election is something I relish, but running every two years for the U.S. House of Representatives, starting in 1974, it seemed that we were always involved in a campaign.

The year 1987 was going to be special for another reason. Sheila had set a wedding date with Perry Knop for September 12. I had all kinds of plans to help her make this the kind of wedding she wanted. Our home, built in 1981, needed additional landscaping. I wanted to oversee that personally. Sheila finished her last semester of law school at Southern Illinois University. She had taken a semester off from Georgetown Law School to help Paul in 1984 and decided to conclude her courses at SIU. She took the Illinois State Bar examination in February 1987 and passed. In April when Paul announced, she was an attorney for the Land of Lincoln Legal Assistance office in Carbondale. While I served as a consultant for the American Association of Retired Persons doing legal research on retirement communities, I felt that I could combine my work in Washington with time on wedding preparations in Southern Illinois.

Really, a full-time presidential campaign was not an appealing prospect!

Someone has said there are a hundred possible candidates for the presidency in the U.S. Senate. Paul was not one of them. As a first-term senator, he wanted to get established with his committee assignments and get his personal agenda for Illinois in the works. Almost every weekend he returned to Illinois for town meetings and hearings. Offices in Chicago, Springfield, Carbondale, and East St. Louis were busy, and the needs of Illinois were great. It was an exciting time, and the six-year term was the icing on the cake. But the talk continued about him as a possible Democratic candidate in 1988. Our friend, Senator Dale Bumpers of Arkansas, had briefly considered becoming a candidate in 1984 but never made a formal announcement. This time he appeared to be getting ready to actively seek the Democratic nomination for president, talking to finance people and possible campaign managers; making speeches in various states, including Iowa and New Hampshire. Paul pushed him to make his formal announcement and enthusiastically welcomed his entrance. Paul admired Senator Bumpers's grasp of issues, his forceful stand on civil rights as a Southern Senator, his approach to government. Paul and I were eager to help his campaign in any way. To set matters at rest regarding Paul's possible candidacy and to encourage Senator Bumpers, Paul called a press conference on February 27, 1987, to say he would not become a candidate for the Democratic nomination and that he fully supported and endorsed the candidacy of Senator Bumpers.

This happy state of affairs lasted only until March 20, 1987, when we learned that Senator Bumpers, following a knee operation, decided that he would not be able to conduct a presidential campaign. I learned of his decision from Martin who heard it on the radio. As soon as I was aware of this news, I knew that Paul's name would once more be mentioned.

Not that there existed any lack of Democratic candidates. Congressman Richard Gephardt of Missouri, had been working in Iowa, the first state to hold a presidential preference test, for almost two years. Senator Joseph Biden of Delaware had a staff in Iowa. Governor Michael Dukakis's folks were increasingly active. The Reverend Jesse Jackson had been pursuing the nomination for four years. And Senator Gary Hart led in the polls. Did the Democratic party need another candidate? Many people in Illinois and elsewhere thought so and strongly urged Paul to become a candidate. Letters, phone calls, and personal visits of delegations urged Paul to reconsider, to be a candidate in the tradition of Harry Truman, Hubert Humphrey, and Franklin D. Roosevelt, a champion of civil rights dedicated to the interests of the average working American and especially to the needs of the growing "underclass." County chairs in Illinois urged Paul to be a candidate. Teachers and union leaders joined in an appeal to him. It was difficult to think of anything else, and difficult to come to a decision.

Some days I thought of all my plans for the year, Sheila's wedding, and maybe a vacation trip for Paul and me. Martin was doing well as a photographer, with free-lance work and stringing for the Associated Press in Washington. Why interrupt all this to run for president since we knew, based on our Senate campaign experience, that this would again be a full family effort with separations, long days, and many nights in motels, with speeches to give and coffee parties to attend?

And always there was that uncertainty, not knowing if we

were doing the right thing and worrying about campaign financing—always a problem with us. On those days I would tell Paul that I'd be just as happy if he were to pass up this great opportunity. Then there were other days when I considered his remarkable career—starting out at age 25—by winning a seat in the Illinois General Assembly against formidable odds, his election as lieutenant governor in 1968 with a governor of another party (unique in Illinois history), and his amazing victory in 1984—and I would think, "Why not Paul?" Finally, with the Easter recess approaching, Paul and I had an opportunity to spend a weekend in Boca Raton, Florida, to make a decision. The weather being unpleasant, we had no excuse to delay any more. Difficult as it was to be objective about my husband, I knew that Paul wanted my candid opinion. He didn't want me to say, "whatever you want to do is fine with me." This had to be *our* decision.

Trying to approach this task in a careful, constructive way, I reached for a yellow legal-size note pad to jot down the pros and cons.

"You're a new Senator, Paul—won't your constituents in Illinois resent this?" I asked.

"Republicans undoubtedly will, but I believe I can do more for Illinois from the White House than I can in the Senate," he answered. "It's a risk any officeholder takes."

I remember our friends in the Twenty-second Congressional District who didn't want Paul to run for the Senate in 1984 for the same reason—they thought he would lose his effectiveness for Southern Illinois. They changed their minds after his election to the Senate.

"We know what it's like to be separated for days and sometimes weeks from our 1984 experience; this time we will insist on a day together at least once a week," Paul said, anticipating one of my chief objections.

"Can we ask Sheila and Martin to interrupt their lives again?" I asked. Paul and I agreed it was their decision. "What about money? This will take so many millions, and you know how tough it was to raise $5 million in the Senate campaign," I said.

"No doubt about it, that's a problem, but if we can get a good lift off in Iowa, it should be easier," he answered. The answer to the biggest question of all—Can we run a good campaign, discuss the issues realistically, and make it all the way?—finally came down to a gut feeling.

"Go for it, Paul," I said.

"We will," he concluded. The hardest part was over.

The details of putting a staff together, finding a campaign manager, answering all the mail, and accommodating the pressures of the press took more time than I thought they should. I wanted to get to Iowa. Finally, the announcement was made that would change our lives for a year, that was to give us unforgettable experiences (and some quite forgettable), and to help us realize the strengths and weaknesses of our primary/caucus system for nominating a president.

Returning to Paul's office after the announcement on April 9, we found the hall jammed with more reporters and TV camera crews, waiting for one-on-one interviews. I was happy to see Mike Jackson, Channel 7 in Chicago; Mike Flannery, Channel 2 in Chicago; our old friend, Hugh Hill from ABC; Carol Marin from NBC; and Dave Stricklin from Channel 12, CBS in Carbondale.

It was in response to a question from Carol Marin that I first articulated my feelings about the term "First Lady." Carol asked how I felt about the prospect of being the "First Lady," and I frankly stated that while I looked forward to the White House for Paul and me, I did not care for the term "First Lady."

"It seems to be decorative and a put-down of other women, and I would simply like to be known as the president's wife," I said. She looked startled. For the rest of the campaign, almost every time I was interviewed and the term "First Lady" was used, I gave the same reply. In the David Frost interview in September at our home in Makanda (more about that later), I explained that the title appeared to be a hold-over from colonial days and our British ancestors, that if I wanted a title, I would earn it, as I had my law degree and my seat in the Illinois General Assembly. He looked startled as well. I wanted to make it clear from the start that my role in the campaign for the nomination and, if it were to happen, my role as wife of the president, would be an active one, not ceremonial, speaking to the issues in a forthright way that women in America would understand and appreciate. It is possible to be a totally supportive wife and still be an individual, even in the heady atmosphere of a presidential campaign. The women that I met in the months to come understood what I was saying and frequently nodded in approval. But some reporters, in a condescending way, often inquired what my "big project" would be if I were the First Lady. When I mentioned that I had several concerns, including passage of the Civil Rights Restoration Act, the health and safety of coal miners, adult illiteracy, extension of library service to small communities, pay equity for women, quality child care with federal standards, and the reunification of families agreed to by the Soviet Union in the Helsinki Accord but never carried out, they seemed disappointed that I was not going to concentrate on one item. Maybe I should have talked about recipes.

At least one person in California felt strongly enough about my remarks on the David Frost show to write and tell me that while he thought Paul did very well in the interview:

> The one negative note on that interview was the almost strident image you project. We all know that you are an independent and accomplished woman . . . but MY GOD do you have to come across like 15 wild horses galloping across the stage?

Watching the late news in Washington on April 9, it was encouraging to hear among the announcement news pieces that Paul had a good chance to "emerge from the pack" in Iowa.

Ever since Jimmy Carter had used Iowa as a springboard for his nomination bid in 1976, conventional wisdom decreed that candidates should diligently pursue the Iowa delegates since the Iowa caucuses are first in the nation and get an inordinate amount of press attention. We believed that wisdom and planned to spend the Easter recess in Iowa, starting April 13.

By February 8, 1988, the date of the Iowa caucuses, we were to spend many days in its ninety-nine counties; to drive for hours seeing little else but rows of corn in the hot summer; to face bitter blizzards when ice on the wings of our charter plane made flying hazardous; but, most of all, to get to know the folks in Iowa who were well prepared to face any candidate for the presidency with tough questions and great hospitality.

As I look back on a solid year of campaigning and ask myself, "Would I do it all over again?" The answer has to be yes—even with the disappointing, but necessary suspension of Paul's campaign a year later. It was the quintessential experience for two politicians.

★ 2 ★

The Campaign Begins—
Iowa and New Hampshire

Y ou can't sleep late on the first day of a campaign, whether it's for state representative or president, so I was glad Paul had to face the TV camera, instead of me, for an interview at his Senate office at 7 A.M. I drove him in our old Chevy from there to the Hay-Adams Hotel for one of *Christian Science Monitor* reporter Godfrey Sperling's famous breakfasts for journalists.

"Are you sure I'm invited?" I asked Paul on the way over. He assured me I was, but truthfully I don't think he knew.

A jammed room greeted us when we arrived—a good sign— and we knew many of the people there. Paul's friendship with Mr. Sperling goes back to their early days in Springfield, Illinois. He is in the category of "OFOP," an acronym the campaign staff in 1984 coined for all the "old friends of Paul" who were in every one of Illinois's one-hundred-two counties.

The questions were tough but not hostile. Paul barely managed to finish a cup of tea when they started. As a former newspaper editor and publisher, Paul usually has a good relationship with the press. Where I tend to see a bias or want to give a snappy answer to a stupid question i.e., "Do you really think, Mrs. Simon, that your husband has a chance to get the nomination?" Paul is patient. While I enjoyed the fruit, eggs, and croissant, I resolved to try and improve my responses to reporters. There will be a lot of them, I thought, and I'd better start now.

23

With Easter recess about to begin, we reviewed the schedule. Several months ago, we had contemplated a visit to South Africa. Paul is Chairman of the Senate Subcommittee on Africa of the Foreign Relations Committee. Iowa now became our target. With Floyd Fithian, Paul's administrative aide and about-to-be-named campaign manager, and Kathy Inboden, his scheduler, we worked out a full five days in Iowa while munching tuna salad sandwiches in his office. We also squeezed in one day in South Dakota and two days in New Hampshire.

Floyd is a former congressman from Indiana, elected in 1974 with Paul, who lost a senate race to Senator Richard Lugar in 1982. Floyd's experience in having been in a major campaign, his knowledge of the issues, and long friendship with us, made it seem inevitable that he would be campaign manager, although he preferred to remain as head of the senate staff. We met Kathy in 1982, a student at Southern Illinois University who volunteered in the congressional campaign and then came to Washington to work for Paul in the House. Her Southern Illinois roots and knowledge of all the players in the downstate counties were important in planning the schedule for our trips back home to Illinois.

Scheduling is a tricky business, requiring great skill. As we planned our first campaign trip to Iowa, we worked with the Iowa Democratic Party, and we learned of events that were "musts." We made calls to set up meetings with various organizations—peace groups, teachers' organizations, and labor unions. These were natural constituents of Paul's. We finally got it all together.

Before our first day in Iowa, we stopped in Chicago to visit my mother in a nursing home. She is frail and has a decided memory loss. I don't see her often and thought it best not to tell her that Paul was a candidate for the Democratic nomination for president. My brother Bill Hurley and his wife, Sheila, met us at O'Hare Airport, excited about a warm, friendly Roger Simon (no relation) column in the *Chicago Tribune*. Recalling a day he spent with Paul in the 1974 Congressional campaign that ended in Frogtown, he wrote that Paul met a woman who indicated that she was deaf. To Roger's surprise, Paul used sign language to say "I'm happy to see you," and got a warm response. I also have used that simple phrase in meeting someone with a hearing disability and wish I could communicate more.

"Kup's" column in the *Chicago Sun-Times* speculated about where the true sympathies of Mayor Harold Washington lie, with Jesse Jackson or Paul Simon. Paul's friendship with the mayor went back to the days when they were active in the Young Democrats. They also served together in the Illinois Legislature and the U.S. House of Representatives. Several items in the Chicago gossip columns had hinted that the mayor would prefer to endorse Paul, not the Reverend Jesse Jackson. Paul and Jesse Jackson have known each other for a long time also. I remember Jesse when he wore a dashiki and an "Afro." I also remember that Jesse did not support Paul in his Senate race in 1984. But Mayor Washington stood with us on El platforms the day before that election urging the voters to go for Paul.

After our visit with my mother and late in the evening, as Paul and I walked along Michigan Avenue back to our hotel— always a beautiful stroll but especially this night—we enjoyed the first taste of public acclaim as a presidential candidate. Paul has held office in Illinois for more than thirty years and is frequently recognized with his trademark bow tie and horn-rimmed glasses. That night, I sensed that people were proud of him and they wished him well. Taxi drivers, young people, police officers, shopkeepers, people having dinner who happened to look out the window shouted, "Go for it, Paul," "Way to go, Senator," or gave him the thumbs-up sign.

Before we left for Iowa, we met with old friends and supporters from past campaigns who promised to raise money and organize for us. Bob Gibson, President of the Illinois AFL-CIO, gave Paul his personal endorsement. We were counting on strong support from friends in Illinois, although we knew that several candidates had been to Illinois seeking help, particularly in Chicago and Cook County.

On the plane with us from Chicago to Des Moines for Paul's first press conference in Iowa we saw Mike Briggs of the *Chicago Sun-Times* and Dick Kay, NBC-TV in Chicago. Waiting to greet us in Des Moines was Berkley Bedell, newly retired congressman from Iowa's Sixth District, now a strong Simon supporter, willing to devote a year of his life to help Paul. The press conference was spirited. National and local media were there, as well as members of the Iowa Democratic Party's board of directors. Surprisingly, there were no questions about the poor state of the farm economy.

In the audience, I sat next to an older man who represented the "notch babies," a well-organized group of retirees born between 1917 and 1922, who believe they have been treated unfairly because of a comparative loss in Social Security benefits through a congressional readjustment. I talked at length with him and assured him that Paul knew of this hardship and awaited a General Accounting Office study due soon. However, the man did not want an expression of interest and concern, but an outright promise to restore fully the lost amounts, which would cost many billions of dollars. Notch babies remained active throughout the campaign and a few of them even threatened to disrupt a large televised forum with all the presidential candidates present.

Single interest groups always have the potential to be unreasonable and to completely ignore other aspects of the candidate's platform. In this case, Paul's sponsorship in the Senate of a bill to provide for long-term home health care for older persons was an exciting prospect that held limited interest for the notch babies.

While Paul met with John Crystal, a prominent Democratic banker, and later with labor leaders, I made a quick trip to the nearest men's store to buy him an underwear supply. He frequently leaves home without some essential item since he takes about five minutes to pack a bag, whether for a trip home to Illinois or to the Middle East. Later in our campaign journey, raincoats had a way of disappearing. We wound up buying three for Paul, including one expensive Burberry when there was no other choice.

Two old friends from Illinois, David Bybee and John Gianulis, were at the Savery Hotel in Des Moines to greet us. For pols, the Savery was *the* place to be in Des Moines. The lobby and bar were fully occupied with politicians of both parties, the media, and staff people for the major presidential candidates. One could sense an aura of excitement when Senator Joe Biden walked in, and Jules Witcover and Jack Germond joined him for dinner. Instead of having dinner at a reasonable hour (lunch never did make it on the schedule), we opted for campaigning at a nearby bowling alley, a favorite place of Paul's in congressional races. David Bybee and John Gianulis went with us. Both the proprietor and the bowlers were more than willing to stop for a moment, put down a can of beer, and shake hands with the newest entry in the presidential sweepstakes. Competing with the roaring noise of balls rolling down the alleys, we nevertheless greeted everyone there.

In the months to come, we found that bowling alleys were good places to meet people and a good way to get on the evening news. Paul didn't have to say anything of substance but he looked good! A bowler I am not, although I was at one time a member of the Law Department of the Brunswick Corporation in Chicago and I always looked for the Brunswick logo on the alleys.

Our April days in Iowa went by quickly in a blur of campaign stops. With Floyd Fithian and a local volunteer or two, Paul and I drove to dozens of counties meeting local Democrats and statewide officeholders. At many of the stops we were joined by Berkley Bedell.

Berk had made a complete recovery from Lyme disease (his reason for not running for reelection in 1986) and was eager to get going in Iowa. Berk's wife, Elinor, and I had been friends ever since we met in the early days of the Ninety-fourth Congress, when Berk and Paul first came to Washington as part of that large Democratic contingent known as the "Watergate Class."

Elinor and I had worked on programs for the Ninety-fourth Club of Congressional Wives. We organized visits for our members to places of interest in Washington and shared in the mutual support system that keeps so many new congressional wives from feeling left out as their husbands fulfill their important roles in the Congress and back home. Information on baby-sitters, day care, part-time job opportunities, how to get along with your husband's staff, and a lot of practical advice was exchanged at our meetings.

"The Wives" developed a bond of sisterhood over the years that had particular significance as we faced more campaigns and the possibility of losing the next election.

Elinor and I also shared an interest in Peace Links, an organization started by Betty Bumpers, the wife of Senator Dale Bumpers, and devoted to informing women on issues of war and peace. Elinor had organized many Peace Links groups in Iowa. I had tried to do the same in Illinois but not with as great success.

Paul and I were fortunate to have the all-out support of the Bedells since they were so well known and respected in Iowa. As we worked our way through countless breakfasts, coffees, luncheons, receptions, and dinners, Berk's warm, personal, thoughtful comments about Paul's career and what his presidency would mean were perfect for the Iowa audiences who knew Berk and trusted him. At their beautiful home overlooking Spirit Lake, the Bedells held a successful fund-raiser for our campaign. People would say to me, "If Berkley Bedell says your husband would make a good president, that's good enough for me." And they meant it!

Most of all, I watched Paul as he plunged into the demanding role of a candidate seeking the nomination of his party. I had no illusions that it would be easy, but I now realized the intensity of each appearance. With the media following closely, each answer had to be weighed. He had to be ready to comment on events on the national as well as international scene. He knew his answers would be compared with the other candidates, all of whom, with the exception of Senator Al Gore of Tennessee who announced a few days after Paul, were well ahead in the polls.

I was beginning to get the "feel" of his campaign, as Paul stressed the need for better educational opportunities, especially for preschool children; long-term care for the elderly; arms control; reducing our federal deficit; and offering a vision for our country of full employment, and equal opportunity for all. These were all goals he had pursued as a member of the U.S. House for ten years and now as a U.S. Senator. He knew what he was talking about, and that made a big difference.

Except for major occasions, Paul never read prepared speeches. He preferred to read from notes on the back of an envelope, and kept eye contact with his audience. Although he seldom told a joke in the usual way of most politicians (sometimes I wished he would), he used self-deprecating humor and involved his audience by calling some of them by name, especially if there was a child sitting up front. I wondered how I would do on the stump. It wouldn't be too much longer and I would be out there, *alone*.

I first sensed what a difference there is in running for the U.S. Senate and a presidential nomination at our first evening reception at the home of Cleone and Leo Menage in Webster City. This was typical of many gatherings to come, a fund-raiser for the Iowa Democratic Party where the candidate was the honored guest or drawing card. While the party solicited funds from the local Democrats, we had an opportunity to meet and speak to people who, in all probability, would be going to the caucuses in February. What distinguished this meeting was the presence of national press.

Jules Witcover, the syndicated columnist, was drinking a cup of coffee in the kitchen. In the living room I met two *Time* magazine reporters and one reporter from *U.S. News & World Report*. And, in addition, there were local newspaper and radio representatives.

I introduced myself to everyone, chatted with them, and then sat on the floor of a crowded living room to hear Bonnie Campbell, the efficient chair of the Iowa Democratic Party, introduce Paul. Her introduction was well researched and fair. She had to maintain neutrality, although her husband, Ed Campbell (a former Iowa Democratic Party chair), strongly and openly supported Dick Gephardt.

Following Paul's remarks, the audience was ready with tough questions revealing more than a superficial knowledge of the U.S. trade deficit, the rural economy, Supreme Court nominees, and many other topics. He received warm applause (to my great relief) when he concluded. While not rushing to get on the almost nonexistent Simon bandwagon, many there said they would like to receive more information as time went on and gave us their names and addresses.

"It was a good start, Papa," I said in the car on our way to Waterloo.

As we moved around the state, we met former classmates of Paul's from Dana College (in Blair, Nebraska) and friends from Illinois who had moved to Iowa. The mayor of Davenport, Thom Hart, went all out with an enthusiastic endorsement and held a reception at his home. Finally, we met David Yepsen, chief political correspondent for the *Des Moines Register,* at a stop in Storm Lake. I would have preferred for David to meet Paul at a big rally with a lot of supporters. Instead, a small crowd waited patiently to hear him. Paul surprised me and everyone else when Dick Vavroch, a former Illinoisan, asked Paul how he could ever keep in touch with the people if he were president.

"Will you have town meetings as president, as you do in Illinois as senator?" Dick asked.

"I will," Paul said. "And the first one will be in Storm Lake, Iowa!"

At a well-attended 7 A.M. breakfast in Mason City with local and national press, the manager of the Country Kitchen said, "Some guy from Delaware [Senator Joe Biden] didn't have as many people here last week." Little remarks like that can do a lot for the morale of the candidate's wife.

I have a picture of Paul with a farmer at a farm near Spencer—in a hog pen! We had to do it, I guess, but it did seem contrived. Joanne and Bob Fahnlander were extremely cordial (arrangements had been made in advance for this "photo opportunity"), but I had to laugh at Paul wearing a borrowed plaid shirt and chasing little pigs around the pen for a good picture!

I decided to pay more attention to farm legislation and the farm economy and learned to be comfortable with words like "parity" and "set-asides."

With all the national attention that Iowa receives every four years as the caucus date approaches, I assumed that most Iowans would be somewhat knowledgeable about the parties and candidates. Not so!

Desperate to get my hair done, I stopped at a salon in Davenport. I introduced myself to the young operator and casually mentioned that I was there to help my husband in the Iowa caucuses.

"Tell me more about it," she said. "I don't read the newspapers or watch news on TV." Over the loud blasts of the blow dryer, I tried to bring her up to date. At the same time, I realized she was most likely not registered to vote nor likely to attend the caucus. I hoped that there were not too many people in Iowa with that lack of interest.

Before we returned to Washington, we stopped in Chicago to keep some commitments made long before Paul's decision to be a candidate. In the company of several plainclothes police officers, we visited Cabrini-Green, a large housing project named for an Italian saint and a former Illinois governor (a rare combination) and the scene of much violence, gang warfare, drugs, and despair. The neighborhood is desolate. It lacks even the usual amenities of a housing project such as outdoor play equipment, benches for older persons, and a few trees or shrubs. Most of all, it lacks hope.

Former Chicago Mayor Jane Byrne, during her incumbency and to her credit, lived there for a couple of weeks, enduring the lack of heat, poor elevator service, roaches and rats, and experiencing the feeling of hopelessness that the tenants share. We met officers of the tenants' association and attended one of their meetings. Lawyers at Cabrini-Green Legal Clinic work with the tenants' association to provide some relief in landlord and tenant problems. Some tenants believe they can make improvements at Cabrini-Green, and we applauded their efforts.

With a great feeling of relief and dead tired, we returned to our Washington apartment late in the evening, stopping at Paul's Senate office on the way to pick up a big box of mail and clippings. At home, Paul made popcorn in the microwave, his sole culinary accomplishment. With the popcorn and Pepsi, we read all the papers and stacks of mail. I received two invitations: one from Peace Links inviting me to join a two-week tour of the Soviet Union in August; the other, from Congressional Wives for Soviet Jewry (one of my organizations) to go to Vienna, Austria, in June for five days. We were to meet with representatives of countries that were signatories to the Helsinki Accord, including the Soviet Union. My immediate reaction was to decline both, citing the urgency and need for my presence in Iowa, but I decided to hold off on a definite answer for a little while.

Easter Sunday, April 19, would be a busy day, so I went to early mass at St. Dominic's. Later in the morning, Paul attended Lutheran services at St. Matthew's. While we often attend two church services at each other's church on Sunday, that day we went alone.

Married prior to Vatican II, we had dealt with the roadblocks of a "mixed marriage" (anathema to Lutherans and Catholics alike) in a practical fashion by acknowledging the validity of each other's faith and trying to worship together whenever we could. We made sure that our children, raised as Catholics, had an opportunity to meet people of many different faiths and tried to broaden their and our understanding of religion and its application to daily life. (Sheila, as a three-year-old, wished the bride and groom "mazeltov" at a Protestant wedding ceremony, having learned the phrase at a Jewish wedding.) This Easter there just wasn't time to be together in church. Laundry and grocery shopping had to be attended to before we left for New Hampshire that afternoon.

In New Hampshire, we were fortunate to have the help of Bob and Frances Shaine, old friends from Hubert Humphrey days. They put together a schedule on short notice that included a stop at the famous Manchester newspaper, the *Union Leader*. With an invitation from Chub Peabody, a former governor of Massachusetts, Paul spoke to a Rotary Club luncheon in Nashua. It was a conservative but attentive audience.

By this time we both were fighting colds, with Contac pills and hot lemonade, but nothing worked. In a campaign, I knew, the schedule continues at all costs. To have the candidate sneezing, blowing his nose, and feeling achy is not helpful to the cause, but we continued.

We met with state legislators in Concord and a former candidate for Congress, Bert Cohen, in Portsmouth. Michael Dukakis, the next-door governor of Massachusetts, cast a large shadow in New Hampshire where his opposition to the Seabrook Nuclear Power Plant made him a hero. He also enjoyed the added advantage that the Boston TV market covers almost all of New Hampshire, so he is a familiar face. I wanted to say to those folks, "Governors are fine, but what is needed is someone with a good working knowledge of foreign affairs and how the federal government, the Congress, and the executive branch work together—someone who can hit the ground running. In short, someone like Paul Simon!"

Coffee with Mary Louise Hancock, a descendant of the famous John Hancock, was a must for candidates in New Hampshire. It is a tradition that each Democratic hopeful visit with her, meet her friends, and seek her blessing, and so we did. Richard Cohen, a *Washington Post* columnist, suggested that she was looking for a candidate with "magic." Paul's magic consists of substance, conviction, and integrity.

On April 21, we celebrated our twenty-eighth wedding anniversary with a quick toast at Boston's Logan Airport. We had hoped to have at least dinner together, but our plane was late and the airport restaurant was closed. We bought a bag of potato chips and later, when we landed in Washington, we picked up two cheeseburgers at McDonald's for a very hungry Floyd Fithian. Anniversary dinners and other family milestones would be on hold for a while.

Paul and I looked back on a solid week of campaigning for the most important job in the free world. It was exhilarating to see what we had accomplished. We were going to have to play catch-up with the other candidates, but none appeared to have a lock on the nomination. The opinion polls confirmed that. For now, we needed campaign literature, a Washington headquarters, a staff in Iowa, and a small staff in New Hampshire. In short, we needed many things. But it would all come together in time. Our plans now focused on a formal announcement date, May 18, in Illinois and Iowa, and May 19 in Alabama, Georgia, and New Hampshire.

The campaign was indeed under way.

★3★

May 18

We had less than a month to choose the site and make arrangements for the formal announcement, with all the usual trappings of national coverage and a fly-around to the early caucus and primary states.

I also faced the reality that I was committed to several speeches in Illinois and activities with organizations in Washington, scheduled a long time ago. Meal planning and grocery shopping became haphazard, and I often loaded the washer late in the evening. Our son Martin responded to calls from the AP photo assignment editor while Paul came and went to New York, South Carolina, Missouri, or Illinois. We began to leave long notes for each other on the refrigerator and bathroom mirrors.

Increasingly, I longed to be home in Makanda with Sheila, who was working for the Land of Lincoln Legal Assistance Office, to help her get our home ready for the expected influx of guests and press for the May 18 formal announcement.

Speaking to a symposium of the Human Resources Management Association in Chicago on Paul's Guaranteed Job Opportunity bill, I made no mention of his presidential aspirations. I didn't have to. At the luncheon table, several women said they listened to me while thinking of me as "First Lady." Pat Weir, President of Encyclopedia Britannica (U.S.A), also a speaker at the symposium, said, "You would be a first in the White

House—a professional woman with her own insights and background."

In Petersburg, Illinois, I spoke to a meeting of Democratic women, where it seemed that each woman there wanted a picture of me, and I autographed their programs. Shirley McCombs introduced me as "the wife of our next president." It all sounded good, but I knew I was home in Illinois. It definitely would not be the same in Iowa and New Hampshire!

In Washington, I attended Senate hearings, one on home health care and one on mine safety, and took notes so I could discuss these topics knowledgeably with current information. As a board member of the Washington Visiting Nurses Association, I had a special interest in proposals to help organizations that furnished home care to the indigent and needy. A recent mine fire, which killed three miners in Wilberg, Utah, underscored the need for stronger enforcement of federal mine safety regulations. Our home area in Southern Illinois has seen many mine disasters that could have been prevented.

The Democratic Wives Forum invited Joan Mondale to speak on her campaign experiences in 1984, and her life as wife of the vice president. As I listened to her, I recalled what a good job she had done for Fritz in a tough year. Could I do as well? In thanking her on behalf of our group, I said she was a role model for us all.

Reluctantly, I told Betty Bumpers that I could not leave the country for the two-week Peace Links visit in the Soviet Union, although I wanted to join the delegation and meet Soviet women. Paul and I spent some time in Moscow and Kiev in 1981 as part of a congressional delegation. However, the spirit of "glasnost" in the summer of 1987 would make this a much different occasion. When I told Dolores Beilenson, wife of Congressman Tony Beilenson from California and one of the leaders of the Congressional Wives for Soviet Jewry, that I didn't see how I could go to Vienna in June, she urged me to rethink my answer. She added that Jill Biden, Joanne Kemp, and Jane Gephardt would be in the delegation. It didn't take me long to decide that I would be there, too.

Right on top of returning to Washington from that trip, I was scheduled to speak to one section of the American Library Association convention in San Francisco on federal library legislation and small-town libraries, long an interest of mine. I could feel the jet lag already, but it all seemed worthwhile. The Illinois Library Association had also promised an honorarium, which I don't receive often.

George Will, columnist and former Illinoisan, requested an opportunity to interview Paul, which was quickly arranged. Although he is known for his conservative bent, we believe he has a genuine interest in Paul. Many years ago, Paul spoke to his high school class in Urbana, Illinois. With every desire to make Mr. Will comfortable, Jackie Williams, Paul's Senate secretary, inquired as to his breakfast preference. Dry toast and crisp bacon, we were told, and that is what the Senate Dining Room provided. He sported a bow tie, as did Paul. Every time he wanted to write down an answer, he whipped out a fountain pen, unscrewed the cap, jotted down a few words, and then carefully recapped the pen. I was fascinated to watch him work.

His column entitled "Bow Tie Politics" appeared May 11, 1988, in *Newsweek*. He observed:

> Simon's ambition is (as was said of Lincoln) a little engine that knows no rest. That is true of all who rise toward the presidency. Something not true of all is true of Simon: he is ambitious to do something, not just to be something.

Another columnist, David Broder, wrote in April 1987 that there is a new breed of candidates' spouses "who are likely to redefine the concept of the candidate's wife in 1988 and of first lady in 1989." Mentioning Tipper Gore, Liddy Dole, and Kitty Dukakis as women of accomplishment and experience in government, he went on to say:

> Jeanne Simon was an Illinois legislator when she married her husband, Paul, now Senator from Illinois and a Democratic presidential hopeful. She is also an author, an activist on issues from arms control to library funding, and almost last year's Democratic candidate for lieutenant governor.

Seeing my name and all those good words in a nationally syndicated column made me all the more aware of my need to be fully cognizant of the issues and ready to meet reporters' questions with an adequate answer. I requested and received all the briefing books that Paul had, plus up-to-date material and analyses of events as they occurred. But the staff could not provide the time to read and digest all those documents.

While all the candidates and their spouses were striving to make national news talking about the future of our country, the headline grabbers were Jim and Tammy Bakker, whose private lives featured illicit sex, greed, and extravagance, wholly at variance with their pious religiosity on their "PTL" TV show. In the next few weeks, an even bigger scandal would be top news when the Gary Hart/Donna Rice story broke. In the meantime, Hart moved his headquarters to Denver. His vacated Washington headquarters were now the Simon headquarters located in an old building near the Senate. Hart made his formal announcement in Colorado.

Back in Illinois our daughter Sheila, her fiancé Perry, and I drove to "downtown" Makanda to check out a possible outdoor site for our official announcement May 18. Our little town, population 402, has a United States Post Office, an ice cream shop, and several artisans (weaving and stained glass) in the "business" section. We also have a monument to "Boomer," a dog that prevented a train wreck by timely barking many years ago when trains were frequent in the valley. There is a special charm here, but there is no grocery store, no cafe, and no town square. Our town's most illustrious citizen is Wayman Presley, ninety-five years old, who, when he retired as a rural mail carrier, started a travel tour agency that is now one of the largest in the United States. As a lone dog crossed the main street (the only moving thing in sight), we decided that Makanda would not do to accommodate the crowds, bands, and media we expected on May 18.

Perry suggested the steps of Shryock Auditorium on the campus of Southern Illinois University in Carbondale, about twelve miles from our home. It is an old historical building where President William Howard Taft gave the first lecture in 1917. University officials were more than happy to let us use the facility and added that we could move indoors in case of rain.

When Paul called that evening from Iowa, we were happy to tell him about our plans for Shryock but shared his disappointment to learn that a *Des Moines Register* poll gave him 1 percent and Gary Hart a whopping 67 percent. Jesse Jackson was also doing well. Biden, Gore, and Simon were all at the bottom of the poll. With the stories beginning to circulate in the press about Gary Hart and a woman at his Washington townhouse, I predicted his 67 percent wouldn't last long. Paul urged me to "get to Iowa" and start my part of the campaign surrogating soon.

Before joining Paul in Iowa, I drove to Springfield to speak to the Central Illinois Women's Bar Association at its joint professional dinner. To my great delight, Judge Jeanne Scott told me that the turnout was the biggest they had ever had. They even had to turn people away! On my way home to Makanda, I stopped in Freeburg and spoke to 200 school children on the subject of drug abuse, using Nancy Reagan's theme of "Just Say No." It was not a political talk, but later several teachers told me they were supporting Paul strongly in his presidential bid.

On May 7, Paul's mother, Ruth Simon, Sheila, Perry, and I looked on while Sheila was admitted to the Illinois Bar. We were saddened only by the fact that Paul could not be there to congratulate her too because of a key vote in the Senate. She is the third generation in our family to be admitted to the Illinois Bar. My father, Ira W. Hurley, was the first in 1916, and we are proud of her.

All that day the news was of Gary Hart and his withdrawal from the presidential campaign. What will it mean to Paul and the other candidates? We wondered. The next *Des Moines Register* poll would be quite different.

Paul and I caught up with each other at O'Hare where he was surrounded by TV cameras and reporters, all wanting his reaction to the Gary Hart story, not with questions about his own campaign. Paul and Senator Hart had been colleagues in Congress. Lee Hart is my friend. It was difficult to frame an answer that didn't sound judgmental. Obviously this would be the only topic for reporters for days to come, and the preoccupation with this story didn't help us at all.

It was good to get back to Iowa and put in a long day of campaigning with Berk Bedell. We ended the day at a huge Polk County steak fry at the fairgrounds in Des Moines, the first big Democratic rally of the season. Gephardt and Biden fans were all over the place with big signs, stickers, and T-shirts proclaiming their choice. Busloads from Missouri, we were told, swelled the Gephardt crowd. I only wished that there was a busload from Illinois to make our presence felt. With one staff person, Chuck Pennachio, who sat behind a card table with a hand-lettered sign saying simply "Paul Simon," and a few mimeographed copies of Paul's biography to distribute, we were simply not competing on a par with the other candidates. Maybe we made a mistake to come here, I thought to myself, without signs and literature. Undaunted, Paul and I stood at the long food line and introduced ourselves to each person as they stood waiting.

The acoustics were terrible, and the restless crowd didn't help. Long, energetic cheers from the faithful greeted Senator Biden and Congressman Gephardt when they were introduced and whenever they paused for breath. What would they do when Paul was introduced? I wondered. I got a sick feeling in my stomach thinking he might be greeted with a minimum of cheers.

Paul's turn at the microphone came, and I joined him while he introduced me. I said "Good luck, dear," kissed him, and left the stage to listen from the floor. The crowd responded to his introduction with some enthusiasm, but not on a par with the other candidates. The background noise of many conversations made it difficult for us to hear him. But Paul was not deterred by the noise and continued with his remarks. Many TV cameras were on a wide platform in front of the podium so there was a larger audience than the one in this building. Ken Bode of

NBC-TV asked me to join him for a brief interview when Paul finished. I mentally prepared myself for tough questions, but all Ken asked was "What will Gary Hart's withdrawal and the press scrutiny of the candidates and their families mean to you, Mrs. Simon?"

"I have no fear for Paul and me or Sheila and Martin, but I am concerned that someone might learn that Grandma Simon made wine in the basement," I answered with a smile.

Press scrutiny is a factor of political life, and we had nothing to hide. Paul is the only member of Congress who has disclosed in detail his income every year for thirty-four years, far more detail than the law requires. As the campaign went on, reporters often asked questions that probed our lives, trying to elicit some unusual feature. Only one reporter, in Concord, New Hampshire, irritated me when he wanted to know details about the adoption of our son, Martin.

"None of yours or anyone else's business," I replied. There is some "right to privacy" for candidates.

Early the next morning, I extracted the Sunday *Des Moines Register* from the box outside our motel room to read what they had to say about Paul. Not too much in the story, but worse than that, there were pictures of every candidate *except* Paul! This was indeed a letdown, but it was my birthday and Mother's Day, and we had a full day of campaign stops ahead of us.

After Paul and I attended mass at St. Ambrose and services at St. John's Lutheran Church, a block away in Des Moines, we left for meetings in Jefferson and Boone. The very small turnout at each one made us question the wisdom of scheduling events on Sunday. In this case, Mother's Day just made it worse. The Busy Bee Cafe in Jefferson was anything but busy. Our announced arrival drew only a handful of people who didn't seem to be all that happy about being there.

Tim Landis, a reporter from the *Southern Illinoisan*, traveled with us. I wanted him to write glowing stories for our friends back home in Southern Illinois to read.

At the next stop, Boone, the birthplace of Mamie Eisenhower, about twelve people gathered at a small cafe to listen to Paul. At the conclusion of his remarks, during which he touched on arms control, social security, and the sale of arms to the Ayatollah, he called for questions. Now we'll see what folks in this small, rural community have on their minds, I thought, and hoped there would be some penetrating questions. The first one was a surprise.

"Tell us something about yourself, your parents, your children, where you come from," an older man said. He really wanted to know about Paul Simon, the man, not Paul Simon the Senator or the candidate. It was a valuable lesson. In some ways we had to start all over in Iowa, just as if Paul were running for his very first office. Folks in Iowa were not as familiar with a Senator from Illinois as we might have assumed. Later on, after all the debates and months of campaigning, it would be different. But in the beginning, a little background was important for every audience.

An evening reception in Ames, the home of Iowa State University, was an outstanding success, with many students and faculty gathered at a home and an ABC-TV camera crew taping. Throughout the campaign, college and university audiences were a source of strength for us. As we met students all over Iowa, New Hampshire, Minnesota, and Wisconsin, whether they were from the state universities or private colleges, we found willing volunteers who made great contributions in time, enthusiasm, and zeal. What was it about Paul, the oldest candidate, that inspired these students? Hard to say, but they loved him.

We ended the day in Des Moines with a dinner for two. Happy birthday, happy Mother's Day, and happy campaign day! This made up for the twenty-eighth wedding anniversary at Logan Airport.

As we approached the formal announcement date of May 18, increasing frenzy was evident. In Washington, I wound down my activities with the Visiting Nurses Association, the Democratic Wives Forum, and my International Club, explaining that I would probably not be at their meetings for the next few months.

Much needed to be done in Makanda. The grass needed attention, the landscaping had bare spots, the windows were dirty. We had invited the press and media to an open house on the day before the announcement, and I wanted our home to look its best. Furious furniture polishing, window washing, grass mowing, sweeping, and vacuuming took place. Ruth Simon, Paul's mother, joined us and pitched in with a dust cloth. When Paul arrived, it looked ready for any visitor, but he barely noticed. He took a quick swim before he practiced his speech with a teleprompter. Perry cooked the bluegill and large-mouthed bass he and Martin had caught in our lake that day, and after dinner Sheila played her banjo. How good it was to be together!

Tim Landis's piece in the *Southern Illinoisan* headlined "All You Want to Know about Paul Simon" was the highlight of the Sunday paper. Our open house was from 3 P.M. to 5:30 P.M., but it ended at 7. A tidal wave of TV, print, and radio journalists arrived, causing a cloud of dust on our little country road and probably driving the deer back into the forest. Paul and I sat on the deck, walked out on the dock, and around our home, trailed by cameras and microphones, doing our best to be ourselves.

Time and *Newsweek* magazines, the *Los Angeles Times*, and the *Atlanta Constitution* were there as well as the *Chicago Tribune*, *Chicago Sun-Times* and many others. There were television cameras from around the nation. The day could not have been better for weather, for the perfect setting, and for the good feeling everyone seemed to have.

Only one small incident marred the day—a phone call from a disgruntled person in Carbondale who had some problem with a disability claim. As I jotted down his name and telephone number so a staff person could help, his language became abusive and he demanded that Paul do something immediately. He talked about a hunger strike and possible suicide, and I got the impression that he might cause some disturbance or harm when Paul was speaking. A call to Sheriff Kilquist reassured me that the authorities knew all about him and were prepared to deal with him if necessary. Paul dismissed this incident as he has similar incidents over the past years. It occurred to me that his increasing visibility might well encourage more of this activity. The good news was a *New York Times* poll showing Paul with a respectable 6 percent, number three after Jesse Jackson and Governor Dukakis.

We canceled our plans for an outdoor announcement ceremony at Southern Illinois University when a prediction for rain came early the next morning. We didn't question the wisdom of our advance men as they quickly put the alternate indoor plan into action.

From our first glimpse of the campus in Carbondale, I knew that we would have a big crowd. An hour before the starting time of 9 A.M., cars, vans, buses, bicycles, and motorcycles were bringing people in. High school bands were practicing outside. A huge U.S. flag over the entrance to Shryock Auditorium was a beautiful sight. Inside and backstage we greeted Neil Hartigan, Attorney General of Illinois, who would be the master of ceremonies, Congressmen Dick Durbin and Lane Evans, and many state legislators. The mayor of Carbondale, Neil Dillard, told us President Harry Truman spoke there in his famous 1948 campaign, and that seemed like a good omen to us.

The auditorium was packed, and hundreds were outside when the program started. Neil introduced Paul's mother, Sheila, Martin, Perry, and me. One by one, we walked out on the stage to deafening applause. Neil's introduction of Paul built up to a magnificent crescendo of emotion that erupted when Paul walked to the podium. The whole place went wild with band music, cheers, yells, and applause. People were holding up handmade signs, "We Love Paul," "Paul for Prez," "Kids for Paul." As he acknowledged this tumultuous welcome with waves and smiles, I had a hard time not crying, just for sheer joy. Instead, I hugged Martin and Sheila. Looking at that picture, even today, with Sheila's green dress and my old red suit (a veteran from 1984) brings tears to my eyes. There were frequent interruptions of applause for lines like "Let's send students, teachers, and Peace Corps volunteers to Central America, not weapons," and "Harry Truman wore a bow tie, horn-rimmed glasses, leveled with the American people, and he won." Bob Scheiffer of CBS-TV later said he had never seen such a warm, enthusiastic send-off to a candidate as the one Paul received.

After his speech, we went outside to greet the people there and found old friends from our former home in Troy. After Paul took over the ownership of the failing Troy weekly newspaper at age nineteen, the town saw his rise from editor and publisher to state legislator, lieutenant governor, member of Congress, and senator. Even their high school band was on hand. The rain never came, but the day was warm and humid. The indoor setting was much better for all of us.

With seventy-three members of the press, we left the Southern Illinois University airport to make the same announcement in Indianola, Iowa. Indianola High School welcomed the opportunity to involve the students with the actual beginning of a presidential campaign. Again, the bands, posters, and decorations gave the right atmosphere, and a panel of students asked Paul questions. Then we headed back to Carbondale for what promised to be a gigantic fund-raiser at the university.

The welcoming crowd on the tarmac at the airport looked like all the pictures we'd seen of the arrival of presidential candidates. Paul and I shook every hand that reached out from behind the fence. One county chairman, Martin Humm, was clearly carried away with exuberance as he stood on the fence holding on to a post with one hand in a most precarious position and waving with the other. Would there ever be another day as much fun, with such an air of excitement and expectation as this? I doubted it.

The overflow crowd at the dinner contributed about $100,000 to the campaign fund, and again there was that important feeling of pride that whatever else may happen, our friends in Illinois had great confidence in Paul. There could not have been a better way to end the day than by saying thank you to them for all they had done for us in the past and promise them that we would work hard to justify their faith.

A charter jet took us to Birmingham, Alabama, at midnight. The day had far exceeded our expectations in enthusiasm and media coverage. When I picked up the *New York Times* the next day, on page 1 I saw a picture of myself adjusting Paul's bow tie.

Birmingham, Alabama; Atlanta, Georgia; and then Manchester, New Hampshire, in quick succession gave us three more formal announcement opportunities. Paul began the press conference in Manchester by commenting on the firing on the frigate, USS *Stark* in the Persian Gulf. He expressed sympathy for the families of thirty-seven Navy men and criticized the administration policy that sold arms to Iran and gave intelligence to Iraq.

Any hopes for support from a previous host Bert Cohen ended with his decision to go with Dukakis. State Representative and Minority Leader Mary Chambers of the New Hampshire House of Delegates was also strong for Dukakis. Attending a dinner in her honor in Concord, I found a politeness on the part of the Democrats I met but nothing more. Nevertheless, our small New Hampshire staff, Kathy Saltmarsh, Gary Galanis, Jim Coish—and especially Bob Shaine—felt there was a good chance to come in with a strong second to Governor Dukakis.

As we headed back to Washington, I knew it would be difficult to wind down from an excellent beginning, the glitz of TV, Lear jet transportation with our family, and red-carpet treatment. As we relished reading the press clips (good pictures and good stories, both) in the *Washington Post* and Chicago papers, we knew the more grueling work of the foot soldier had just begun.

★4★

On The Road and on My Own

Before I could begin to campaign in Iowa, as much as I wanted to, Floyd Fithian had other plans for me. He proposed a series of Illinois mini fund-raisers, which would also give us media attention. Since our entry into the presidential contest had not been in the making for months or years, as with some of the candidates, and lacking family wealth or an ethnic base of support as others had, we looked to those who had been with Paul over the years for financial support. We were not disappointed.

The rising expectations of our friends were buoyed by yet another national poll. The NBC/*Wall Street Journal* poll showed Jesse Jackson at 14 percent, Governor Dukakis with 10 percent, and Paul with 9 percent. This was the third consecutive poll showing Paul in third place, and he had just started! I knew polls can be deceiving and give false encouragement, but it pleased me to share the good news at meetings in many downstate Illinois cities and towns—Effingham, Mattoon, Shelbyville, Charleston, Danville, Salem, Rantoul, Kankakee, Streator, and Champaign.

With Ellen Sinclair and Jo Alice Pierce driving and making arrangements to meet local Democrats and press, we started off by raising $5,000 in our first day. Those and other funds we raised were matched in January 1988 under the matching

47

funds program administered by the Federal Election Commission. Such success on our opening day went to our heads. We couldn't believe we did so well. Jo Alice and Ellen also conducted a brisk sale of buttons, posters, and Paul's books. My picture was on the front page of the Charleston paper—in color! I kept telling myself that we were in Illinois, after all, where people knew and had voted for Paul, but I had not expected such a willingness to make the financial sacrifice that this entailed.

The days were long and full. A breakfast reception at a law office or home was followed by still another coffee party. A luncheon was preceded by several radio and newspaper interviews. We were in farm homes and homes with fine antiques, small cafes and college campus watering holes.

In one three-hour period in Danville, we managed to have nine media events and a large luncheon, organized by an old friend, Paul Manion. Paul rushed me so much that I had only two bites of chicken before I stood up to speak. As we left town, I asked Jo Alice to stop at a drive-in so I could get something to eat!

For all the events that we attended where food was in abundance and, in many cases, specially prepared, it was difficult to eat since I really wanted to talk more than eat. It's hard to carry on a meaningful conversation and eat a meal at the same time. If I did take a bite, someone was sure to ask me Paul's position on our naval forces in the Gulf of Hormuz or a similar weighty question, and I would swallow quickly and reply. I pretended to eat and hoped that the host would offer a bag of goodies to carry in the car as we drove to the next stop.

At the end of our first swing, I noticed that I could take in my belt one more notch—a painless way to lose weight! I recalled reading that Lynda Johnson Robb used to put a roll in her purse at a banquet in case the waiter should remove her plate too precipitously while she was in conversation. All the old jokes about having a piece of parsley stuck in your teeth took on a new meaning when I faced a television camera with no opportunity for a quick mirror check. The days in Illinois seemed so much like our 1984 Senate campaign that every now and then it seemed unreal that Paul was a candidate for president this time.

As we moved around Illinois on our fund-raising tour, I began to appreciate the feeling of pride people had in Paul and their desire to participate in the often maligned system we have for choosing a presidential candidate.

Young people wanted to be involved and were organizing trips to Iowa for a weekend or a week to help the cause. At the University of Illinois at Urbana, we had an absolutely great event—a beer and pretzels party with students and faculty at a modest admission price. Although I was tired when I walked into Treno's Restaurant at 7:30 P.M. and said to Jo Alice, "Let's just stay for an hour," we didn't leave until long after 9 and then drove eighty miles to Kankakee, arriving at midnight. The thrill of identifying people who were committed to Paul, eager to work, to write to friends and relatives in Iowa, and to contribute dollars as well, brought a rush of adrenalin that wiped out my fatigue.

Like a performer on stage, a politician (or a politician's wife) needs that recognition that comes from genuine applause, and I tried to give my audience some applause lines—Paul's opposition to the tax "reform" bill, his support for student loans, his sponsorship of help for handicapped legislation. Sometimes I know I spoke too long. Like many people, I am always uncomfortable before I start to speak and relax when I get going. Usually, I speak much too fast so I made an effort to slow down.

In my first experience at public speaking many years ago, as a candidate for the Illinois General Assembly, my brother Bill stood at the back of the room and made hand gestures to signal "slow down" or "louder." What he couldn't tell me was how to acknowledge applause gracefully the first time I received it!

On the road and alone at night, whether in a motel or at someone's home, I wanted to hear from Martin, Sheila, and Paul to find out how their day had gone and what the latest hot news was. Sometimes when I heard from Paul long past midnight I waited for a phrase that indicated good news: "Do you have a pencil?" or "Did you hear the news?" The former meant that another poll showing Paul doing well would be released the next day, and Paul wanted me to get the figures in case I didn't see the newspapers.

After all those good days in Illinois, I was in a great mood to win friends for Paul in Iowa. Our small but growing staff there had an excellent scheduler in Ann Mulholland, a veteran of a campaign for Congressman Frank McCloskey of Indiana. She arranged for a driver, and we set off bravely to towns not familiar to me to meet Iowa Democrats (and Republicans, too, I hoped) like a missionary in a foreign country, convinced of the truth of my message and ready to give it my best shot. Small towns like Winterset, Creston, Clarinda, Osceola, and Lamoni were my first assignment.

We were told a few key people were important and able to swing large blocs of voters. Whether true or not, we simply could not afford to bypass them, so they were the designated first stops in the town or county. Not surprisingly, these folks were on every candidate's list, and we found that they had been visited many times by all the other candidates prior to our arrival. Flowers and candy were given to these important people, along with luncheons and dinners, as a part of the courting process, and they expected no less from me. Most of the time, they were genuinely interested in learning about Paul, and sometimes they were kind enough to tell me that they had chosen a candidate already. There were disappointing meetings, such as the Democratic women's luncheon in Winterset where I had a hard time getting a few words in about Paul, but I learned a lot about the local scene. Some considered a former active supporter of Gary Hart in Creston quite a catch, but she was hard to figure out, and I sensed I had not made a convert.

Meeting small-town newspaper editors and publishers was more rewarding. Paul's background as a former editor and publisher of fourteen weekly newspapers in Illinois gave him an added cachet. Ready with Paul's biography, as well as mine, I gave pictures to the editor in case a photographer wasn't handy. Ed Sidey, editor of the paper in Greenfield and brother of Hugh Sidey, the *Time* columnist, had a Republican orientation but was generous in his time with me. Greenfield, a typical small farming community, was the headquarters for Jesse Jackson's campaign, but I didn't see much activity there. A reporter at the paper in Clarinda thanked me for stopping by, but she definitely had no interest in either an interview or a picture. Some editors would talk only to the candidates and could not be bothered to talk to their wives. We left our press release and hoped that they wouldn't throw it away. Women reporters frequently wrote stories about the "wives" as a group but wanted a large chunk of time for the interview.

At a luncheon in Indianola with a group of teachers I spoke earnestly about Paul's record in the field of education, his support for education for people with disabilities, and his service on the education committees throughout his legislative career, as well as his endorsement by Illinois teachers in other elections. They were interested but not to the point of signing up.

All in all, I concluded the folks in Iowa were a hard sell, and I was somewhat discouraged by my initial efforts. This was not like campaigning in Illinois! Getting familiar with elected Democrats, community leaders, "peace" people (Iowans had an intense interest in peace issues) took time. They had to be cultivated slowly.

Sometimes I met a genuine Paul Simon fan, like Dr. Bill Russell at Graceland College in Lamoni, who took me around to the newspaper office and arranged a dinner to meet some of his colleagues. Later in the campaign Paul held a student rally at Graceland, playing off the theme that the "other" Paul Simon had made popular with his "Graceland" album.

Requests for interviews started to come my way. I recall standing at an outdoor telephone for almost half an hour talking to a *USA Today* reporter while trucks rumbled by. When I read the story some days later, I was happy to see that the paper quoted me in the opening paragraph in a page 1 story about the "wives." *USA Today* reporter Mireille Grangenois Gates quoted me:

> "The day of the political wife wearing a large, white orchid waving 'Hello,' and smiling to the crowd is gone forever," says Jeanne Simon, a lawyer-peace activist who is married to presidential hopeful Sen. Paul Simon, D-Ill.
>
> "I don't want to be standing there like a flower on the wall. And I don't want to be used," says Simon. "I don't want to be there just because I'm his wife."

While I continued a planned schedule through Muscatine, Washington, Burlington, and Mount Pleasant (all in Iowa), I felt comfortable speaking for Paul at a labor rally in Keokuk and was bolstered there by the help of Don Johnston, who took a few days off from his position on Paul's Senate staff to help me out.

The last stop in Iowa before going to New York for an appearance on the "CBS Morning Program" gave me the best reception of the whole tour. In Iowa City, the home of the University of Iowa, I met many students and faculty members eager to help Paul. This was more like Illinois, and I relished the chance to tout my candidate.

"Always be respectful of the other Democratic candidates" was a maxim Paul and I adhered to; but that didn't stop me from stressing Paul's background at the state and national level, his foreign travel and Foreign Relations Committee service, his upset victory in 1984, and the possibility of bringing Illinois into the Democratic victory column with twenty-four electoral votes for the first time since 1964—none of which could be matched by other candidates. Student groups from the University of Iowa later gave Paul a rousing welcome at many rallies and went door to door for him in surrounding counties. I began to appreciate university and college campuses as a source of positive Simon support.

My activities and scheduling were managed in the early weeks by Paul's campaign scheduler, an added job for her that took second place to the candidate's needs. This sometimes resulted in inadequate notice to me or the person I was to meet, no press releases on hand, or too many events crowded into a long day.

I needed a staff person or persons whom I could rely on to plan a good schedule with a minimum of advance work and to give me a day with Paul every week. Lea Sinclair, the daughter of old friends from Salem, Illinois, worked in the campaign press room but volunteered to head my staff. She was my only staff for a while. As a former television talk-show host in New Orleans, with a good background in communication skills, she set out to coach me for my first national television appearance.

With mixed emotions I agreed to fly to New York to be interviewed by Mariette Hartley on the "CBS Morning Program." Mixed, because I realized what an audience CBS has and I feared I wasn't ready for this exposure so soon. Arriving in New York at midnight and tired after a long day, I looked forward to a hot bath and bed, but Lea had other plans. We rehearsed all the possible questions and answers with Lea taking Mariette Hartley's role. Lea emphasized that my opening statement should stress the significance of the latest ABC poll, no matter what Ms. Hartley should ask. At 2:30 A.M., I felt reasonably confident that I could start off saying, "Thank you, Mariette. I'm delighted to be with you today, and I'm so excited about the latest poll that shows Paul Simon gaining ground."

At 6:45 A.M., when the CBS limo picked us up, I was anything but confident. I wore my good luck red suit (good luck from the 1984 campaign) and borrowed a white silk blouse from Lea. After a makeup session, I signed a CBS release form, drank lots of coffee, and envied singer Connie Stevens and her two daughters, also guests on the morning program, for their calm demeanor while waiting in the green room. Finally, at 7:25 A.M., I met Mariette whom I liked instantly. I felt ready for my big moment on national TV! I did manage to make my opening statement as we had rehearsed, and I'm not sure what we said after that, but Lea smiled as I walked off the set after the five-minute interview. Mariette said "well done" during a short break, and I felt an immense sense of relief. Dick Wade, a professor at New York University and an old friend from Illinois, joined us at the studio and he loved the interview. I dashed out to call Paul in Washington but couldn't locate him. Others in his office reassured me that I had hit all the right notes. A breakfast later with a reporter from the *New York Times* was almost anticlimactic.

As the campaign progressed, I felt more and more comfortable with television cameras but always a bit tense for national television, such as ABC's "Good Morning, America" or NBC's "Today Show."

I celebrated with a shopping spree on Seventh Avenue—a pink silk suit, a navy blue linen dress, and two skirts, which I convinced myself were needed. Actually a campaign does call for a great variety of suits and dresses, and they have to be suitable for television. I'm fond of tweed skirts and cashmere sweaters in the fall, comfortable cottons and linens in the summer, and silk dresses for the dress-up occasions. (At home in Makanda I wear Oshkosh blue jeans, Martin's old shirts, and my Barat College sweatshirt.)

Now, Lea said, the colors should be strong, no checks or plaids, full skirts for graceful descents from airplanes. Packing and unpacking didn't help the appearance of my wardrobe, and I seldom had the opportunity to use an iron. Fashion maven Richard Blackwell gave up on Paul and me, saying, "Thank heaven they have each other. That's all you can say." I had never heard of Mr. Blackwell before or since, but I hope I meet him some day and clue him in on the problems of looking well-groomed and presentable when one is on the road most of the time.

Nedean Sparks, the owner of a small dress shop in Carbondale, came to my rescue with cotton-knit dresses in teal blue, sage green, and warm pink, that had full skirts, pockets, long sleeves, and a turtleneck. They were a lifesaver to my wardrobe, no matter what Mr. Blackwell may have thought. I do remember seeing an AP wirephoto of me in Maine wearing a sweater designed more for warmth than looks, but Maine is cold in February!

More fund-raisers in Illinois continued to be successful, even in Republican strongholds like Freeport, Oregon, DeKalb, Dixon, Rochelle, and Belvidere. In Freeport, I received an urgent message to call Sheila and was relieved to learn that she only wanted to talk about wedding details.

We made plans for her wedding in a series of phone calls late at night from Iowa, Washington, or wherever I happened to be. I promised her a few days in Makanda when I could really nail down the caterer, florist, and photographer. Sheila chose my wedding dress of twenty-seven years, which pleased me and saved a few hundred dollars.

In return, Sheila promised to make me a dress for her wedding. I chose a Vogue pattern in green linen. Sheila worked in Carbondale, going to Iowa with Perry on weekends to campaign, planning her wedding in spare time, but enjoying every minute of the fast paced days.

Back at our Washington apartment where Martin and Paul had left piles of papers, briefing books, laundry, and luggage, I looked forward to a day off and a dinner date with Paul before he left for speeches in California. He was positively ebullient at our dinner at La Brasserie, and I felt more confident than ever hearing what he had been doing and the endorsements he had picked up. Although I spent my free day doing laundry and straightening up an untidy apartment, I read the *Washington Post* the *New York Times*, and caught up with the news. I haven't had someone to help with our cleaning since our children were small but it occurred to me that this would be a real help now. A friend promised to see what she could do. While Martin did the cooking, I wrote fifty thank you letters, organized my collection of clippings and issue statements, and got ready for the next assignment—a visit to the Wisconsin Democratic convention in Stevens Point to represent Paul.

Paul's family on his father's side is from Wisconsin. They are dairy farmers and clergymen, terribly proud of Paul, and eager to help the campaign. Ed Garvey (a candidate for the Senate) and Uncle Henry Simon met me; and former Congressmen Al Baldus and Bob Cornell were also on hand to introduce me to their friends. I spoke at a breakfast meeting and to two caucus groups—the AFL-CIO and teachers, getting a good reception from each one. The teachers were aware of Paul's record, and the labor group was enthusiastic.

At the labor caucus I followed Governor Dukakis who gave a good, solid talk and said the right things but failed to get applause at any point until the end of his remarks. When I spoke, I stressed my own labor record in the Illinois General Assembly, in particular, my vote against the so-called "right-to-work" bill, and recited Paul's record of support for labor and the fact that he once belonged to the Typographical Union. I gave them something to applaud and they responded. Ed Garvey and Uncle Henry were happy. I also gave a major address to the delegates in which I stressed Paul's Wisconsin roots and his progressive/liberal record. I felt I did well there and at a press conference later. Interestingly, many delegates had seen the CBS Mariette Hartley interview and liked it.

"I saw you on TV" is a magic sentence, a great conversation opener. Most of the time the content of the interview is forgotten but the identification remains. Women particularly liked my comment about Eleanor Roosevelt and Rosalynn Carter as First Ladies who supported their husbands in a substantial way and who were role models for me. The CBS interview gave me much-needed confidence. Reassurance is a welcome commodity.

With the Congressional Wives for Soviet Jewry (including Doris Matsui, Jane Gephardt, Anne Bingaman, Ellen Armstrong, Rosemary Boulter, Myrna Cardin, Chris Sarbanes, June Miller, and Martha Sundquist), I left Washington National Airport for Vienna on the afternoon of June 22. An earlier delegation went to Moscow—Dolores Beilenson, Teresa Heinz, Wren Wirth, and Joanne Kemp—and joined us in Vienna.

Immediately on arrival several of us went to the plenary session of the Committee on Security and Cooperation in Europe where the Soviet and Yugoslavia representatives made predictable speeches but failed to explain why they could not live up to their agreements for the reunification of families and freedom to travel that they agreed to under the Helsinki Accord. We had a "working dinner" with U.S. Ambassador Warren Zimmerman who made reference to Paul's efforts on behalf of Soviet Jewry. On the following days we met with the Canadian, British, Dutch, French, German, Austrian, and Soviet delegations, in each case speaking with the ambassador. The U.S. Ambassador to Austria, Ronald S. Lauder (of the cosmetic family), entertained us at a luncheon at the residence where we enjoyed the ambiance.

Our most moving experience came in a visit to the train station where we met with Soviet Jews who had just left Moscow and were on their way to Rome. They were not allowed off the train, but we were free to board and visit with them. The language barrier could not disguise their obvious joy in freedom at last. We hugged the children, wished them well, and with tears in our eyes said *"do svedanya,"* (good-bye).

A carefully planned presentation to the Soviet ambassador was one of our best meetings. I spoke of the need for a process to let Soviet Jews know all the forms required, timetables, and appeal provisions for applying to leave the Soviet Union and for reapplication after refusal. We also made sure he knew that Joanne Kemp, Jane Gephardt, and Jeanne Simon (the wives of presidential candidates) would be talking to many groups in the United States about their failure to comply.

On the flight back to the United States, I promised myself that I would write my speech for the American Library Association session on "Information: A Social Commodity," but I lacked the necessary discipline to do it.

A day after our arrival in Washington, I boarded a plane to San Francisco. Fighting off sleep, I tried to pull together an outline for my talk. That evening I met with several women activists and my niece, Anne Hurley, to talk about Paul. Late in the evening, and really tired, I made notes on a yellow legal pad and left a call for 5:30 A.M. to finish writing my piece. Somehow it all came together the next morning, as I recalled my service on the Advisory Committee for the White House Conference on Libraries in 1979 and Paul's sponsorship of most of the recent federal library legislation.

I made a point of visiting the public library in each town where I campaigned for Paul, meeting the librarian and inquiring what the Library Services and Construction Act, which Paul had sponsored, meant to their facility. Librarians were pleased to have this attention, and I found it to be a useful form of campaigning. Many Illinois librarians were among those who attended the session at which I spoke. The $2,000 honorarium (the largest I have ever received, by far) helped our modest finances.

After a debriefing at the Chicago Jewish Federation on my recent trip to Vienna, I met Jon Anderson, a feature writer from the *Chicago Tribune* who was doing stories on the wives of the two Illinois candidates, Jackie Jackson and me. *Tribune* photographers spent an hour getting the right pose, then Jon and I left for Makanda so he could get the right background.

Before driving to our home in the country, I stopped at the Federal Building in Carbondale so Jon could meet Sheila, busy with a Social Security hearing, but who took time to visit with him. Although our country road is full of bumps and holes, and we left a dusty trail, our home never looked better as I turned in the driveway. The American flag that always flies there snapped in the breeze, tiny ripples blew across Lac du Simon, and the grass had been mowed. Sheila and Perry had seen to that. If only a few deer had come into view, it would have been perfect.

Anyway, Jon got the picture of an unpretentious, comfortable home, with a vegetable garden, lots of trees and, most of all, peace and quiet. A smoke detector suddenly, for no reason, shattered that peace and quiet, making alarming noises that I had to stop. His story "Running Mates" conveyed a good sense of our family and our home.

> Sitting on her deck in the summer sun surrounded by gray herons, cardinals and blue jays, on a day so muggy and lazy that even the turtles in the pond below are hard-pressed to be snappy, Jeanne Simon, the picture of crisp efficiency, breaks off a chat to take a call from a Washington newspaper. It is, happily, nothing serious.
>
> These are curious times. Presidential aspirants are spotted on yachts in the Bahamas or playing the bongos in nightclubs far from home. Their wives, thrust before the spotlights, are pressed with questions about sexual morality. But Illinois' Sen. Paul Simon is so unlikely a candidate for monkey business that, when the topic comes up, Jeanne Simon merely smiles. She recalls a recent political cartoon in which a reporter spots her bow-tied husband, with a book on Abraham Lincoln under his arm, and asks, "Have you ever committed . . . oh, never mind!"

Sheila, Perry, and I joined Martin and Paul in Houston on July 1, for the very first Democratic debate on "Firing Line," the PBS program. William Buckley had managed to get all the Democratic candidates to agree on this place and time for the nation's first close-up look at the candidates.

All the major networks were there. Backstage, I could feel the suspense building with everyone in our party, except Paul. He exhibited great calm and control as he reviewed notes (no notes were allowed on stage) and had his makeup applied. The makeup woman said he had the best skin of all the candidates! We nervously nibbled hors d'oeuvres, glad that it was Paul and not us who had to face the acerbic Mr. Buckley. Seated in the front row in the auditorium, we joined the families of the other candidates who, presumably, felt as shaky as we did awaiting their appearance.

In magnificent fashion, the moderators—Bob Strauss, former Democratic National Committee chairman served as co-host—and the candidates rose on a platform from the orchestra pit with a small table in front of each on which someone had carefully placed a glass and a carafe of water. I noted that Jesse Jackson had orange juice. We managed to catch Paul's eye so he knew where we were. He smiled and waved back.

Mr. Buckley and Mr. Strauss made introductory statements, and Mr. Buckley led off with the first question: "If you were president, which president's picture (Reagan has Calvin Coolidge) would you have in the Cabinet room?" Paul and the others had been given the question in advance and were prepared. I knew what Paul's answer would be, but he had drawn last place and ran the risk of having Jesse, Joe, Al, Bruce, Dick, or Mike give the same answer. Happily, they gave predictable responses—Roosevelt, Truman. Al Gore named James K. Knox, meaning Polk.

I braced myself as Paul said, "I'd have a picture of a steel-worker, a school teacher, a farmer, pictures of working men and women to remind the Cabinet that they were working for all the people in the United States." He looked at the right camera, his voice was deep and firm, and his answer drew applause—the only reply that did. I punched Sheila, "Dad is going to do all right," I said, and he did. I relaxed and enjoyed Mr. Buckley try to needle the candidates and fail. Paul's closing statement sounded good. He had prepared that as well. And then it was over. We rushed onto the stage for hugs and kisses and congratulations. After an interview on "Nightline" about the Bork nomination to the Supreme Court (Paul is on the Judiciary Committee, and Joe Biden serves as the Chairman) and a visit to the press room, we piled into the limo, slammed the door, and let out the wildest possible yells and cheers to express our joy. We knew he had done well in this first acid test with the television cameras.

The papers the next day confirmed our opinion. We all agreed that no candidate ran away with first prize. Jesse Jackson was more subdued than usual. Joe Biden toned down his rhetoric. Al Gore faced the audience in closing but missed the camera. And, Bruce Babbitt became the real loser. He bobbed his head up and down and looked a little silly.

In the morning a call from the Washington campaign office relayed the good news that Tom Shales, the *Washington Post* critic, complimented Paul: "The bright new star to emerge [from the Houston debate] was Sen. Paul Simon of Illinois, who is also the most unassuming of the bunch. He seemed level headed, forthright and peppery, . . . and, best of all, bracingly Trumanesque." The *Des Moines Register* reported three winners, Simon, Gore, and Dukakis. Evans and Novak said Senator Biden did not do well. They all agreed that the hapless Bruce Babbitt needed some coaching in TV skills. Paul appeared on all the early morning TV shows in Houston after only a few hours of sleep.

It seemed to all of us as we headed out in different directions the next day that we reached an important milestone, a leg up in the first of many debates. Others that followed were not as well organized as "Firing Line," or had as good an audience. First impressions for a nationwide audience are crucial. Paul had clearly proven that he could do all right on television.

★ 5 ★

If It's Tuesday,
It Must Be Keokuk

Our Iowa campaign picked up added momentum with the arrival of Pat Mitchell as Iowa campaign manager, a tough, no nonsense lawyer who had been a Hart supporter in 1984. He added new staff people, planned a statewide coverage of volunteers and staff. Barry Surman, formerly with the *Los Angeles Times,* assumed the job as our press secretary.

I welcomed the discipline Pat brought and got on well with him. He also lost no time in getting me out on the hustings. Congressional district coordinators planned events where we needed strength. As I became friends with the coordinators— Tom Weis, Tim Raphael, Tusha Kimber, Marc Solomon, and Duncan Stewart—I wanted them to do well, especially the ones with hard-core Republican counties. They had the responsibility to get me to the event or to meet someone on time, with literature, pictures, and posters. They called the headquarters in Des Moines at every stop to check for schedule changes and to report on how the Democrats we talked to were "leaning." There were a lot of "leaners" in Iowa.

"Well, I'm leaning towards your husband, but I'd like to know how he plans to help us farmers," or "It's between Paul and Congressman Gephardt (or one of the other six candidates), and I just want to sit down and visit with him for a while."

Paul could not spend all this time with every possible caucus-attendee, but we didn't want to neglect them either. Follow-up phone calls were made by the staff person assigned to the particular county. We tried to get answers to queries back to them as fast as possible.

Paul and I were used to the nomination of candidates by the primary system in Illinois in which each registered voter has the opportunity to vote for a candidate on a ballot, in secret. In Iowa only the caucus-goers could register a choice. However, all voters were eligible for the caucuses and could register at the door of the caucus site. This was accomplished on one evening (February 8, 1988, this year) in homes, halls, fire stations, or wherever—a lengthy process in which a group splits up into smaller groups and makes public declarations for each candidate. If a candidate was not "viable"—i.e., did not have 15 percent of the vote of the entire group—his people had a choice of joining ranks with another candidate or dropping out. After the regrouping, a presidential preference poll was taken, then delegates were elected to go to the county convention, which would then elect delegates to attend the state convention for the final choice. Only the first step in a long process, the caucuses provided the first nationwide straw poll of the strength of the candidates. While Congressman Gephardt won the caucuses by a whisker, Iowa Democrats later voted in the state convention for Governor Dukakis.

If voters told me that they had made up their minds for another candidate, I asked if they would consider Paul as their second choice, in case their first choice was not viable. When Gary Hart, Joe Biden, and Al Gore dropped out of the Iowa caucus (Gore did not drop out but after meeting with little success said he would not campaign further in Iowa, preferring to concentrate on the southern states in "Super Tuesday"), we tried to move quickly to capture those who had been cut adrift. We lost most of the Hart folks but were fortunate to win many of the Biden staff and followers for Paul.

The caucus process was circuitous at best and open to manipulation at worst. If the weather was bad that day, it might be difficult or impossible for some to get to the caucus. There was no provision for absentee ballots, so we lost a few voters who planned to be on vacation in February, as well as those away at school or in nursing homes. They all agreed to vote for Paul in November, but we had to get on the ticket first! Curious Republicans were attending our gatherings. A good sign. But would they come to a Democratic caucus and declare in public for Paul? I doubted it. Bad as it was for us who were not used to it, it made the playing field more level since all candidates had to campaign in person in debates, before groups, and in living rooms. They could not rely entirely on a massive radio and television blitz to persuade voters, although the paid advertising reached astronomical figures for all the candidates by February 8.

As often as possible, we wanted to stay in private homes remembering the great success of Jimmy and Rosalynn Carter in Iowa, where people still brag that the Carters were overnight guests. While this sometimes necessitated artful dodging in the morning for the use of the shower (or I would be in the shower and remember I left my towel in the bedroom), we made some good friends.

Dolores Mulvihill in Clinton heard Paul speak on TV and called up to volunteer her help and her home. I had never slept on a water bed, but hers hit the spot. She did a load of laundry for me while I met with local Democrats she had invited to meet me, individually, so I could make my case for Paul. After a quick lunch with a few friends, I used her telephone to invite people to events where Paul would speak.

We had a good time driving around Iowa, sometimes staying in homes of supporters, sometimes in motels, and occasionally at a "bed and breakfast" that was a real treat. If we were fortunate enough to have a friend or supporter in a small town, it made a big difference.

Dick Vavroch and Kate Rastetter in Pomeroy adopted us and our campaign staff. Tom Weis stayed in a room in a building Dick owned; Kate's homemade pies and cakes were a powerful incentive for hungry volunteers to stop for on the road. Dick's large, comfortable, air-conditioned Cadillac was a decided contrast to our campaign cars. When we were in his area, he always drove me. The Simon campaign cars were old and without air-conditioning. In the hot, sticky summer weather, we tried to stay comfortable by rolling down the windows.

Tusha Kimber, a recent graduate of Grinnell College in Iowa, and I drove an old Chevette. One not-to-be-forgotten day began in Des Moines when my bags did not arrive with me at the airport. We couldn't wait for the next plane and set off for Marshalltown to attend a labor picnic wearing casual clothes.

After the picnic, we drove to Forest City, an uninteresting hundred miles or so on Interstate 35, with hot air blowing in on us. Only a few miles from our destination, a huge bug flew in the car and hit Tusha in the face, causing her to lose control of the car. We crossed the yellow line, went into a deep ditch and out again, drove through a fence and into a pasture, and came to a sudden stop in the front yard of a farm home. Our seat belts prevented broken bones but not bumps and bruises. The Chevette was totaled.

As we emerged shakily from the car, we saw horses running out of the pasture onto the highway. Two young men on motorcycles came along at just the right time and rounded them up. The Winnebago County sheriff arrived on the scene and offered us a ride to East Woods Park where the Democrats of Winnebago and Hancock Counties were gathered. Former Governor Bruce Babbitt was holding forth when I arrived, so I had a few minutes to pull myself together before I made a talk for Paul. In the fading twilight and feeling very sorry for myself, I urged them to consider the merits of the junior Senator from Illinois.

The good news came in the headline in the *Mason City Globe-Gazette* the next day: "Mrs. Simon unhurt in mishap near Forest City." It even made the wires! Bruce Babbitt was also mentioned in the story as an afterthought: "Jeanne Simon was joined at the podium by former Gov. Bruce Babbitt." Some folks in Forest

City thought I arrived at the park on horseback. Our staff said I would do anything for a headline! Shortly after that "mishap," Tusha and I had a better car, with air-conditioning.

My luggage came along late the next day but not in time for church in Estherville. My hostess, Dorothy Mergen, sought out a friend of hers closer to my 5'9" than her 5'3". In borrowed clothes, I spoke at a candidates breakfast after Mass that morning.

Small towns do not have large or well-appointed motels. When Sheila and Perry checked into the Imperial Motor Lodge in Sioux City, the desk clerk cheerfully told them that if their shower had only cold water, to come back and get the key for another room. At the "R" Motel in Gainer, Iowa, I had a feeling that I was in the Bates Motel in the movie *Psycho* as I put a chair up against the door. The next night I was at the Marquette Hotel in Minneapolis, in a splendid room, where I reveled in room service, a huge TV, and a room with a view.

Jim and Evelyn Hodges in Burlington had a beautiful old home where I stayed as a "bed and breakfast" guest. Antique furniture, handmade quilts, soft lights, and a bowl of fruit provided a restful atmosphere. Evelyn's breakfast featured waffles with sour cream and strawberries, link sausages, orange juice, and coffee. Jim wanted to take me to the airport, but I insisted on a taxi. When Sheila and Perry stayed there one night with only a credit card the Hodges could not take, the Hodges waived payment.

There were good days and bad days. A good, responsive audience made me feel that our efforts were really paying off, and then I would hit the wall with others and wonder where I went wrong.

In the basement community room of a small bank in Cresco, the county chair managed to gather a handful of people for coffee, Fig Newtons, and Oreos to meet me. We sat on folding chairs in a small circle. As I like to do, I asked each person's name and tried to find out a little bit about them so I could relate some of Paul's ideas to their concerns. They were unusually reticent, hardly offered a word, listened but had absolutely no questions or comments. They were more like zombies in a "Twilight Zone" episode. I would sooner have downright opposition than silence. Tim Raphael and I were grateful for a telephone call that interrupted the meeting. I returned to say, not entirely truthfully, that we had to leave for an emergency meeting of our staff and left.

I was glad I never had to follow Jesse Jackson after I heard him speak at a dinner in Carroll County. We had made several stops that day, and I was hot and sweaty as we arrived for the dinner. Every other candidate seemed to have more supporters, posters, and literature than we had, but I was assured that I had an opportunity to speak for Paul. I tried to be succinct and hoped the other speakers would also. Hattie Babbitt looked as though she had just stepped out of the shower and wore a beautiful rose linen dress. I followed her and Senator Tom Harkin.

The air-conditioning was not adequate for the great crowd that gathered, but when Reverend Jackson spoke, we forgot that and listened to every word. What a superb speaker, and what a receptive audience he had! I cheered with the rest as he excoriated the administration for its failures in civil rights, education, and economic opportunity for all.

High school classes where the teacher had made some preparation for a discussion were a challenge, especially when some student wanted to make a speech. Young audiences usually reflect the attitudes of their parents so I could soon tell if the pervasive spirit of the community was Democratic or Republican. If the students were eighteen, of course they could participate in the caucuses, so we tried to recruit willing workers in the government, American history, and civics classes. My favorite groups were the college audiences at schools where I did not expect to find progressive Democrats, like Luther College, Coe College, Grinnell, and Mount St. Mary's. Intensely interested in international issues, such as apartheid in South Africa, the INF Treaty, and the Strategic Defense Initiative, they also cheered me time and again for Paul's stand against the nomination of Judge Bork and his "no" vote on the confirmation of Attorney General Edwin Meese.

Senior citizen luncheon sites were usually good places to stop if we arrived before lunch was served. With a microphone, I would make a short statement and then visit each table with literature. The hearty, well-balanced luncheons were usually too big for me, but hungry young staffers appreciated them. Sometimes I observed one or more seniors asleep while I was talking, but then I've been there myself, so I couldn't complain. What I couldn't handle were the conversations that sometimes went on while I was speaking, or when people would talk to me while we were listening to another speaker. Social Security, Medicare, and long-term home health care were their main concerns, along with the lack of housing and the increasing cost of living.

Just as some of the "peace" people wanted nothing less than an all-out commitment to total, unilateral disarmament (which would be foolhardy), some groups pursued a hard line that left no room for compromise or consideration. Some so-called "right-to-life" groups were concerned with the fetus up to the moment of birth but decried any special help thereafter for nutrition supplements for infants and mothers, early educational opportunity, fair housing, or an increase in the minimum wage, all of which make life a little better for millions of Americans. These were, by and large, Republican groups, attending the Republican caucuses.

The Iran-Contra hearings in Congress were the subject of many discussions. The Democrats gleefully watched the Republicans take the heat for this enormous, hard-to-understand folly of President Reagan, Vice President Bush, and the National Security Council, mesmerized by Colonel North. While the nation watched Colonel Oliver North try to explain how he sold arms to Iran in return for aid to the Contras in Nicaragua and defend his abuse of the Constitution, Paul's Senate offices in Chicago, Washington, and Springfield began to receive stacks of mail and phone calls praising North for his patriotism. Colonel North's allies in the conservative right and fundamentalist groups mounted a powerful campaign to let the congressional panel know how they regarded their "hero."

In the middle of the hearings, with public acclamation for North peaking, the National Association of County Officials (NACO) held a convention in Indianapolis, Indiana, and invited presidential candidates to address them. President Reagan and Governor Dukakis preceded Paul.

Listening to National Public Radio on our car radio in Iowa, I heard Paul say to the convention, "Colonel North is not a hero," followed by boos from the audience. I had never heard Paul booed, and I didn't like it. It was not until later that evening at O'Hare Airport when I picked up the *Chicago Tribune* and read reporter Mitch Locin's story of Paul's speech that I felt better. "The boos changed to cheers," he wrote, as Paul went on to say that "Anyone who lied, shredded evidence, had a clandestine operation in the basement of the White House, and did not uphold the Constitution he had sworn to uphold could not be called a hero." He quoted Abraham Lincoln, as a young state legislator in Illinois in 1838, following the death by a mob of Elijah Lovejoy, an abolitionist editor in Alton, Illinois:

> Let every American, every lover of liberty, every well-wisher to his posterity, swear by the blood of the [American] revolution never to violate in the least particular the laws of this country; and never to tolerate their violation by others.

My pride in Paul for taking this unpopular stand with such an audience and making them accept the truth about Colonel North was overwhelming. It took courage that no one else showed to say that.

Later, as the hearings faded into memory, Paul was not alone in his assessment of the "hero." As often as I could, I reminded audiences that Paul's kind of toughness, not the loud-voiced, fist-pounding kind, was needed in the White House.

After my first television appearance on CBS, I felt less apprehensive when Joan Lunden asked me with only a day's advance notice to come to New York for the "Good Morning, America" program to join Hattie Babbitt and Joanne Kemp. I reasoned that appearing with two of the "wives" would be easier. To my surprise, only Joan and I were in the studio. Hattie Babbitt was in San Diego, and Joanne Kemp was at home in Bethesda, Maryland. Talking to Hattie and Joanne, who appeared on large screens, was unusual. Since I was in the studio, I had the advantage of being able to interject comments and exchange more dialogue with Joan Lunden.

At one point in the interview, Joan Lunden dropped her notes on the floor, and I bent over to pick them up. This was Joan's last day on "Good Morning, America" before she took maternity leave, and I knew there was no way she could have retrieved them. After the program, Lea Sinclair told me I should have left the notes on the floor; that I disappeared from the screen for a second or two with no explanation. But Joan Lunden thanked me.

The stump speeches and television appearances, with help from our staff on issues, should have made me feel confident about the "First Ladies' Forum" at Drake University, sponsored by the Polk County Democratic Organization, scheduled in late July. The wives of all the candidates (with the exception of Jackie Jackson) had accepted the invitation. I don't know about the rest of the wives, but as the oldest wife in the group, I wondered how I would do against Hattie, Tipper, Kitty, Jane, and Jill.

I asked for and received two days at home in Makanda to draft a speech, get some rest, and help with wedding plans. Sheila was in Iowa so I had the house to myself. I picked sweet corn in the garden for dinner, arranged flowers, and watched deer splashing in the water. When Paul called from Cleveland, I told him that just for a minute I wished he was not a candidate but with me in Makanda. Tired but happy with his day, he reminded me that we might have more vacation than we wanted if we didn't do well in Iowa. I made phone calls to the photographer and the caterer and talked to numerous friends who wanted a first-hand account of the campaign in Iowa. After securing a piano for the church, I conferred with the church secretary about uninvited guests. With those items out of the way, I took a yellow legal pad out on the deck to get a healthy tan while I worked on my speech. The temptation to daydream was powerful, but I knew that this speech had to be good.

Each of us had five minutes to relate what we would do if our husbands were elected. I decided that a bit of history on the role of First Lady might be in order, using a book Lea requested from the Library of Congress, titled *First Ladies* by Betty Boyd Caroli. It explains how the position of the president's wife has evolved over the years. My role models were Eleanor Roosevelt and Rosalynn Carter, who took an active interest in helping their husbands. Most of all, I wanted to thank the Polk County Democrats for according us this special status as women who could make a contribution on our own.

On the evening before the forum, I practiced my speech with Lea, and on the day of the forum, I must have gone over it twenty times with help from Sheila and Perry on when to pause, when to slow down, and when to smile. I wasn't ready, but the time had come to face not only the audience but the other wives as well. We assembled in the green room for last-minute makeup help, waiting for our moderator, Ruth Harkin, the wife of Senator Tom Harkin, to lead us onto the stage in alphabetical order, the order in which we would speak. It was a break for me. An old political axiom says the last speaker leaves the best impression. It also means a high degree of nervousness sets in while other speakers take their turns.

Jill Biden was accompanied by Senator Biden; Hattie Babbitt had several laugh lines; Kitty was serious as she read her speech; Tipper was forceful in speaking of her fight against pornographic rock lyrics; and Jane said the first thing she would do in the White House would be to put her feet up.

Clutching my notes, I acknowledged Ruth's introduction and

smiled as Sheila, Perry, and many of our staff cheered. Dick Vavroch waved a big ten-gallon hat. They gave me such a good feeling that I regained my confidence and sailed into my oration. There had been no applause for any of the other speakers except at the conclusion, but I managed to evoke several enthusiastic rounds when I talked about the importance of Title IX, dear to the hearts of young women, and thanked the committee for not giving us a big white orchid to wear or asking us to pour tea and, especially, for not asking us to give our husbands' favorite recipes. I finished to a standing ovation, much to my surprise and delight. Only then did I realize that any advantage I had was due to my service in the state legislature, campaigning with and for Paul over the years, and speaking to groups like the League of Women Voters and the AAUW, explaining and advocating legislation, and discreet lobbying with Paul's colleagues. Experience had helped me.

We mingled with the audience, and I spoke to several reporters and received congratulations from a happy staff. The *Des Moines Register* barely noted our efforts the next day, and the *Washington Post* reporter treated the forum as a "ladies' day" event in the Style Section. The real audience were the C-SPAN (Cable Satellite Public Affairs Network) viewers who told me over the course of the next months in the campaign that they were impressed with my talk.

★6★

Sheila's Wedding vs. Paul's Campaign

With the momentum of Paul's campaign in Iowa, New Hampshire, and other states clearly growing and the need to make final wedding plans in Makanda, I did my best to keep a level head and my composure. In this I was greatly aided by the formation of the "Jeanne Team," a small, efficient staff in Washington, headed by Lea Sinclair, with Pamela Huey as press secretary (on leave from Paul's Senate staff where she was deputy press secretary), Patricia Montgomery as scheduler (the most difficult job of all), with help from May Mineta, the wife of a congressman and a dear friend of mine. May would sometimes add a note on the schedule at the end of what appeared to be a long day: "I know this looks tough, Jeanne, but you can do it. You're a congressional wife!"

Their tiny office in the basement of our Washington headquarters was more like a broom closet, jammed with files, desks, and typewriters. Pam wrote a new version of my old biography and a decent picture accompanied it. Lea ordered special stationery with our campaign logo for me. They worked out schedules in advance with names and addresses of persons to contact in the area. They notified the press and scheduled requests for interviews at home or on the road.

Either Lea, Patty, or Pam drove me to the airport or met me, no matter what the hour. They met protests that I could drive my old Mustang myself with fixed opposition. They were determined to take over! I realized that they wanted me to feel comfortable, not to worry about details, and I accepted their more than generous efforts.

With a solid campaign staff now in place in Iowa, it was possible to begin minicampaigns in states that had early primaries and in some states where our Democratic friends just wanted us to get a cadre of Simon supporters motivated. Paul had been doing this, in addition to attending fund-raisers that kept the cash flowing in. Now my turn came to branch out beyond Iowa.

Minnesota held caucuses in February, and we had several friends there. Jerry Soderberg from Minneapolis, formerly a Hart fund-raiser, urged us to get moving across his state. In one day, I made six airport stops with Greg Dahl, a young state senator. He planned airport stops at St. Cloud, Alexandria, Duluth, Mankato, Rochester, and Minneapolis. At each stop we had a well-orchestrated press contingent and sympathetic supporters with signs. In Rochester, I was surprised to see old friends from Southern Illinois. How good it was to look out and recognize Virginia and Bob Otterson. When I asked for questions in St. Cloud, a woman in the front row stood up and said she had no questions, but her granddaughter, Karin Dougan, was a classmate of Sheila's at Georgetown Law School and would be playing the piano at her wedding! Arvonne Fraser, a dynamic leader at the Hubert H. Humphrey Institute of Public Affairs and the wife of Donald Fraser, mayor of Minneapolis, organized a breakfast where I met many women activists.

A reunion with Paul and Martin in Manchester, New Hampshire, was canceled when Paul had to have emergency oral surgery in Washington. I couldn't even get Paul on the phone, but I had my orders—fill in for Paul in New Hampshire. Paul is very stoic about pain, but I wanted to be with him and keep him comfortable.

After a day of street campaigning and radio interviews in Dover and Portsmouth, I met Bill Lambrecht of the *St. Louis*

Post-Dispatch, who was writing an in-depth story about me destined for the *Post-Dispatch* Sunday magazine. His story on Jane Gephardt a few weeks earlier was excellent, and I hoped for equal treatment. I had known Bill since his days as a journalism student of Paul's at Sangamon State University in Springfield, but I could not rely on friendship for a sympathetic story.

When the story appeared, I was more than pleased when I saw a picture on the cover of the magazine and a caption entitled "Jeanne and Paul Simon—Campaigning for the Presidency and Loving It."

The scenery of New Hampshire made my trip there more like a vacation, with the special help of the Shaines smoothing the way. Riding in Bob Shaine's comfortable Lincoln "Shainemobile" spoiled me for more mundane cars. Bob, Bill Delano (a former President Kennedy staffer), and I welcomed workers at 5:30 A.M. in Berlin, New Hampshire, where there is a strong smell of sulfur from the paper pulp mill.

We wound up in Dartmouth where Paul (minus a tooth) joined us at a meeting pulled together by John Rassias, an ebullient professor whose enthusiasm knows no bounds when it comes to the study of foreign languages (his specialty) or supporting Paul Simon.

Before I left for a swing through Indiana, Paul and I had a glorious day at the Illinois State Fair in Springfield. We have been to most of the "Democratic Days" at the fair in years past in honor of other candidates at the top of the ticket. Now it was Paul's day! It was predictably hot, but we were used to that.

The crowds at a press conference, a Democratic luncheon, and at the fair grounds were large and noisy. They had come from all over the state, and each person had to personally tell Paul and me how well it was going for Paul in his or her county or precinct. Former Secretary of State Paul Powell had become well-known in Illinois for the discovery of $600,000 in cash found in shoe boxes in his closet after his death. He sat in the seat in front of me during my first term in the Illinois House. Powell had a colorful phrase for Democrats who sense a winning ticket: "They smell the meat a-cookin'." The Democrats at the State Fair appeared to have caught the scent of a winner in Paul Simon.

They knew him so well. The older ones had been with him many times. He had helped them with appearances in their counties and worked for local candidates. His weekly column, mailed free for thirty years to any newspaper in Illinois that requested it, had also given him recognition. A crowd of reporters followed him as he visited the sheep and goat barns and presented ribbons. Fred Barnes of the *New Republic* wrinkled his nose and stepped carefully as he tried to keep up with the candidate. It was hard to say good-bye to Paul after basking in all that warm feeling of being with people who know you well.

I did not know a soul in Indiana, but before the close of the day I found a surprising degree of support for Paul there. Perhaps that was not so surprising, I reasoned, since the Chicago newspapers are read there, and there is a spillover of radio and TV news. We started in South Bend and chartered a plane there to take us to Indianapolis and Evansville. Mike Marshall, in charge of the day and later to be in charge of the New Hampshire campaign effort, is a former Indiana state legislator. He introduced me to elected officials, union members, and teachers. Our charter plane had one engine and one pilot, and the one pilot had a difficult time starting the one engine before we got going at each airport. Paul's edict of "two engines, two pilots for all campaign trips" had not reached Mike. I felt obliged to carry on, albeit with trepidation.

There is no audience like an audience of labor union members! They love to applaud and express themselves vociferously, either for or against a candidate or a cause. In Salt Lake City, Utah and again in Casper, Wyoming, I spoke to AFL-CIO state conventions and received a very warm welcome. For the first time, I saw the AFL-CIO videotape featuring each of the presidential candidates, Republican and Democratic. Paul's segment was straightforward, not pandering to labor. In fact, he pointed out, he had differed with them from time to time, but was concerned always with the welfare of working men and women. A union member told me, "It's not only that he represents us, he is one of us."

The union leaders were careful not to repeat the mistake of four years ago when they endorsed Walter Mondale early in the primary campaign, making it appear as if he owed them his nomination. Even so, members expressed their sentiments clearly, with hissing and booing for certain Republican candidates and cheers for Paul.

Dave Thomas, a young lawyer in Salt Lake City, organized our campaign as the Mormon Church is organized in Utah— carefully structured by wards and districts. Our friends there included Frances Farley, a state senator, and former U.S. Senator Ted Moss. They drove us to Provo and to the campus of the University of Utah to meet some of the few Democrats in that state.

In Wyoming, we had the help of Jim Bankes, an old friend from Illinois who helped Paul in his first congressional campaign. He was all set to do it again in Wyoming. Leaving Casper, Lea and I met Governor Sullivan in the airport. He arrived without a staff or aides, refreshingly casual and unassuming.

I happily told Paul about Utah and Wyoming when we met again in Des Moines. The staff and I gave him a big welcome as his plane rolled in, exhibiting a growing feeling of a possible win in Iowa. Our apartment in Des Moines was small, but Kathy Roth and Kathleen Murray, two effervescent staffers, had stocked the refrigerator with cream cheese and bagels, Pepsi, popcorn, and wine. Fresh flowers were on the table. Eschewing a dinner in a restaurant, we had a great evening alone.

We were both unable to sleep so we sat in the kitchen, poured ourselves bowls of breakfast cereal and talked until 1:30 A.M. Our one-day reunion was brief. I stayed with Paul only long enough to be with him at a reception the next day in Des Moines.

Marc Solomon, a recent college graduate, had come from

Cleveland, Ohio, to work for Paul's campaign. He was excited to go with me to a rally in Congressman Dave Nagle's district. I came to the steak fry/rally to speak for Paul and discovered that I would follow Senator Biden. When I saw Joe and Jill Biden surrounded by cameras and reporters, I wished Paul were there. A great crowd gathered to hear the Congressman and Senator. I hoped they would hold still long enough to listen to me. The crowded room had no air conditioning. People were drinking, and the audience was standing, for the most part, but the speeches went on. Senator Biden gave a moving talk about his family and his rise from humble beginnings, the same speech that was later to bring about his departure from the presidential campaign, taken in large part from a speech by a member of the British Parliament, Neil Kinnock. My speech was no match for Senator Biden's, but I gave it all the vigor I could muster and even got a few applause lines from a patient audience.

Afterwards, Don Paige, the president of a UAW local, introduced me to everyone there, not allowing me to have one of the steaks that everyone seemed to be enjoying. Both Don and Marc were pleased with my reception. We made sure that we stayed around after the speeches and even found a reporter who wanted an interview. Marc seemed so genuinely happy about the whole rally that it gave me a good feeling, too. I needed to have someone tell me I had done well.

Paul visited South Dakota once, but the Democrats wanted another visit, and the staff tapped me to go. Norma Brick-Samuelson, our Simon volunteer, met me at the airport in Sioux Falls where we had a good press conference, followed by dinner and a talk to members of the National Women's Political Caucus of Minnehaha County. Many of the women there were waiting for Representative Pat Schroeder of Colorado to come to a decision about her candidacy. Paul had an excellent record in support of women's issues, much the same as Congresswoman Schroeder's. I could see a large part of his natural constituency leaving him for Pat Schroeder. Norma and I met party stalwarts in Huron and again at the South Dakota State Fair. We also paid a visit to Hubert Humphrey's pharmacy in Huron, a shrine to the late vice president. Norma was talkative, and I enjoyed her company on the way back. That is, I did until her car abruptly left the road in Mitchell, South Dakota, went up over a curb and jolted to a sudden stop. I nursed my bruises for the next two hours and kept looking at the depth of the ditches along the way, measuring the possible impact until we were safe at the Sioux Falls airport. In addition to my confirmed use of seat belts, I felt that I had a special angel looking after me in campaign cars.

Campaigning with Martin Simon was more like a family outing. We enjoyed bouncing around Oskaloosa, Chariton, and Keosauqua in Iowa with two young staffers, Rachel and Duncan Stewart, stopping at county fairs, voting in straw polls, looking for radio towers, and dropping in at small-town newspapers. Almost uniformly, the local radio stations were delighted to have a guest to interview. Often I jotted down a few questions for them to ask me, and when they asked at the end of an interview, "Is there anything else you would like to add, Mrs. Simon?" I had lots to add about Paul.

Now and then I was a guest on a call-in program, a sitting target for many mean-spirited people with an axe to grind or for an organized assault from friends of the other candidates who, I could tell from the unfamiliarity with the words, were reading from scripts. When the going really got rough, our campaign staff retaliated by phoning in easy soft-ball questions, trying to disguise their voices. But when one caller said, "Your husband is a nerd, spelled n-u-r-d," Martin passed me a note saying, "Tell him he's a jerk, spelled j-u-r-k." If we didn't take ourselves too seriously and could laugh afterwards, the frustration and tension disappeared.

We received plenty of advice and expressed our gratitude, even though we might privately think it useless. How many times did I explain that Paul was not about to start wearing a regular tie (after forty years of wearing a bow tie) just to make somebody happy? Why did he always wear wing-tip shoes? Someone wanted to know (he doesn't); or why does he always look as though he slept in his suit?

Comments about Paul Simon, the singer, confused with Paul Simon, the senator, abounded. I got tired of them. We met people who regarded Paul like prim parents meeting a prospective son-in-law for the first time—very critical of minor points. Even the size of Paul's ears was a subject for comment, as if they had some mysterious effect on presidential decisions. Chinese people hastened to let us know that big ears were a sign of wisdom, and that helped. A reporter from a weekly news magazine who interviewed me disparagingly commented on Paul's ears, revealing, as he spoke, a set of teeth that were unbelievably ocherous. I wanted to hand him a toothbrush but smiled and said "Yes, Walter, Paul does have large ears, but I'm used to them."

The ultimate advice on ears came from a serious woman in Texas who wrote me, assuming I would be grateful to get the word. She said that a relatively minor operation could be performed on Paul's ears. "Just cut off the tips, and he'll look much better." I tore her letter up and threw it away. Minutes later, I started laughing and retrieved it, pasted it together, and kept it for my scrapbook. I guess nothing is sacred in a presidential campaign.

Speech coaches volunteered help on speaking techniques and promised instant charisma if Paul would admit that he had a communication problem. He watched tapes of his speeches and practiced for the ones that would have large audiences but did not feel comfortable with advice from "experts" who had no idea of the needs of a candidate.

"I have to be myself, and to be otherwise, I'd be a phony," he concluded. Since I knew that Paul could bring an audience to its feet with cheers or command silence in a noisy room with his deep bass voice, I wasn't worried about his communication problems—*if* there were any. But earnest ladies wrote and visited me urging me to get Paul to realize that his verbal communication skills were not adequate. How can you explain to a speech coach that each audience is different or that sometimes you can deliver a great speech because you're in the right spot at the right time, or you make eye contact with someone in the front row who is really listening intently.

To have Sheila or Martin say, "Go get 'em, Mom," was all I needed to face a critical audience. If you are tired, you can't make a good talk. You might make a mistake, forget an important point or, the worst sin of all, neglect to acknowledge and thank the person who introduced you and the party kingpins who put the meeting together.

Paul laughed when I told him about the speech expert who told me, in all seriousness, that we should mentally review our speeches, as if on tape, and fast-forward the parts we didn't like. For better or for worse, we had to be ourselves. Audiences want substance, sincerity, and conviction. We tried to give them that.

Our constant travels meant packing and repacking every day, piling up dirty laundry, and looking for one-hour dry cleaners, all of which were a bother but nothing compared to losing luggage. Many times the suitcases arrived on the next plane and were delivered promptly, but on one short flight from Minneapolis to Des Moines my large suitcase disappeared. Northwest Airlines personnel assured me that it would be on the next flight, but it wasn't. For the next two days, I wore the same outfit, rinsing out underwear and hose each night, hoping for the best. In the middle of a meeting in Keokuk, Martin dashed in with a note saying the bag had been located, and I rejoiced. Unfortunately, Northwest sent it back to Washington, the address on my ID tag, and they lost it again, for keeps. The suitcase was a gift to Paul from his Senate staff, and I had appropriated it. It held four dresses, four pairs of shoes, my entire underwear supply, and all my cosmetics. Just replacing all this took time and money. I filled out all the forms to prove my loss, and I received a check promptly.

While the loss of luggage is a headache, our staff hit the panic button when the Boston Airport Ramada lost *me* one evening. Josh King, our young Boston volunteer, met me at Logan Airport at 11:30 P.M. I checked into the Ramada at 11:45 P.M., and I was sound asleep when Lea Sinclair called me at 2 A.M. She had called with a schedule change at midnight, and for two hours they told her I had not checked in and was not there. She notified our campaign manager and the Boston Airport police that I was missing and finally told Paul so he wouldn't hear about his missing wife from reporters! At 2:15 A.M., Paul called from California to make sure I was there and woke me up again! I don't know how they managed to lose a guest, but the embarrassed manager refunded the price of the room, $112.75, with profound apologies the next morning. After that experience, I made sure to see that they duly entered my name on the computer, rolodex, or register.

Leaving the campaign, which was moving well at the end of August, I had no feeling of guilt as I happily contemplated going home to Illinois and putting the finishing touches on Sheila's wedding plans. Paul joined us for one day when the "CBS Morning Program" camera crew and Rolland Smith came to tape a lengthy interview in Makanda, and then Paul hurried back to the hustings. There were more conferences with Lorenzo Cristaudo, who was doing the barbecue for us on the evening before the wedding; with the tent company, on the piano rental; and with the florist. There were wedding presents all over the place. More towels and pillows were needed for overnight guests. I tried on the green linen dress Sheila made for me. It fit perfectly. My wedding dress looked better on her than it did on me twenty-seven years ago.

Only once did I think that Sheila was about to lose her composure—when Paul called to tell her that he would be in a televised forum on educational issues with the Democratic candidates in Chapel Hill, North Carolina, on the afternoon before the wedding and would fly home to Illinois on a commercial plane, arriving just in time for the church rehearsal. Sheila and I firmly told Paul that whatever the expense, it was imperative that he charter a plane to be sure that he arrive in plenty of time. He acceded.

Sheila's college and law school friends arrived the day before the wedding, joining Perry's friends from the Peace Corps. Bill and Sheila Hurley drove from Barrington in northern Illinois. My cousin Marie McDermott and her husband, Tom, who were running our campaign in Pennsylvania, arrived from Philadelphia.

Paul and I were determined not to make a campaign event out of our daughter's wedding, but the presidential campaign crept in nevertheless. The church secretary at St. Francis Xavier and I discussed the problem of uninvited guests. I agreed that no one should be barred from the church, invitation or not, but asked Martin to have the ushers keep an eye out for any strange looking characters. Two well-built ushers said "no problem." Sheila and Perry planned to have their photographer take the usual family pictures in church before the wedding and banned any television or still cameras during the ceremony. In response to many requests, we did allow reporters and TV cameras to come to our home for the barbecue the night before for one-half hour.

About eighty of our friends and relatives gathered under the red-and-white striped tent on the lawn to eat barbecue, listen to bluegrass music, and join in one toast after another of beer, wine, and Pepsi to Sheila and Perry. Perry's parents brought baked beans, salads, fried chicken, cakes, peach cobbler, tomatoes, and cucumbers to supplement Lorenzo's barbecue. The luminaria that we always have at Christmas time (little candles set in sand in brown paper bags) looked just right on a warm, end-of-summer evening, lining the driveway. Determined not to get sniffly, I did get a little moist in the eyes when Sheila picked up her banjo and joined the Wamble Mountain Ramblers. We begged her to sing the song, "Eunice and Pablo," she composed after her first day as an intern in the State's Attorney's office in Jackson County, and we joined in the chorus after each verse. Eunice and Pablo were star-crossed lovers who enjoyed a little gunplay, and Sheila has immortalized them in song.

The church was filled the next day. Law school friends, Pam Chen and Karin Dougan, played the violin and piano as Paul and I walked Sheila down the aisle, preceeded by Janet Thompson, Sheila's roommate at Wittenberg University. When Paul's brother, Reverend Arthur Simon, and Father Jack Frerker from the Newman Center at SIU married them, another Roman Catholic/Lutheran wedding in our family had taken place. At the luncheon and reception at Giant City Lodge, Adlai Stevenson insisted on proposing a special toast to the bride and groom since they met at a Democratic picnic in his honor the year before. Adlai called it the best thing that came out of his ill-fated gubernatorial race, which had been ruined by LaRouche people in the primary.

The pictures in the next day's Sunday paper showed a very happy couple. The best picture appeared in the *Chicago Tribune*. Martin took that one. It would have been ideal if Paul and I could have taken a day off after the wedding, but we had an interview scheduled with David Frost, the British journalist who interviewed Nixon after his fall. Frost filmed interviews with all the candidates of both parties, which would be seen later in the year, hopefully in the few weeks just before the Iowa caucuses. While his camera crew (ten people altogether) took over our home, completely transforming it into a TV studio, moving furniture, putting blue gel on the windows, stringing lights and wires all over, Paul and I were the special guests at a reception in our hometown of Makanda.

Red, white, and blue bunting in the shape of an enormous bow tie covered the upper stories of the shops, a band played, and the Masonic Lodge opened to serve refreshments. Wayman Presley, our esteemed senior citizen, introduced Paul, but paused when a dog walked across the outdoor platform. The event, led by Linda Rowan, the wife of Jeff Rowan, who built our home, got almost everyone in Makanda involved, even some rather dyed-in-the-wool Republicans who declared that "old Paul will do us proud."

David Frost had prepared for the interview with thorough research, having talked to Paul's colleagues and friends, and reading his books on Abraham Lincoln, Elijah Lovejoy, and the Democratic Party. For more than three hours, they talked and got on well with only two or three brief breaks. He also interviewed me and talked about when and where I met Paul, my presidential wife role models, and what my agenda would be in the White House. I enjoyed talking to David. He was disarming, and I loved his British accent. The camera crew applauded when I finished! After a few months of facing TV cameras and reporters, I was much more sure of myself. We were home, and I felt comfortable.

When we viewed the interview in *New York Times* columnist Tom Wicker's apartment in New York in January, I was delighted to see that Paul and I both looked and sounded natural, and the setting was perfect. We had a long day and David Frost had even a longer day, having flown from London to Washington on the Concorde, then from Washington to St. Louis. Then he drove two and one-half hours to reach Carbondale, and was told at the Holiday Inn in Carbondale that he could not have a glass of wine until after noon. To David, it was *already* 5 or 6 P.M.

There were no longer any good excuses to return to Makanda. Perhaps a family reunion at Thanksgiving would be the next time home for all of us. It was back on the road again for Paul and me. Another withdrawal from the list of Democratic candidates—Senator Biden—tightened the race just a bit more. Now there were six: Governor Dukakis, Congressman Gephardt, Senator Gore, Governor Babbitt, Reverend Jackson, and Paul left to battle it out in Iowa and New Hampshire.

★ 7 ★

Rising Expectations

While Sheila and Perry went to Bar Harbor, Maine, for the start of what Sheila said she hoped would be a "fifty-state honeymoon," Paul and Martin left for New Hampshire. My staff produced a schedule for September and October that included fund-raisers in Illinois, a few days in New Hampshire (Mike Marshall asked Paul and me for more appearances), a western swing through Utah, Oregon, Washington State, and Idaho; a southern visit to Baton Rouge, Louisiana; a non-campaign trip to Orlando, Florida, to fulfill a speaking engagement on the U.S. Constitution's bicentennial to a church group; and back to Iowa whenever plans did not take me elsewhere.

While I looked forward to seeing other states and assessing Paul's chances myself, I knew I should be in Iowa because, as we kept telling ourselves, it was "do or die in Iowa." When pressed by the media, we said, "We hope to do well in Iowa." Again, looking at the Carter experience in 1976, the media "bounce" from taking first place in Iowa carries great momentum into New Hampshire and succeeding states.

A campaign runs on money, and our friends in Illinois wanted to help. In Madison County, where Paul started his career as a newspaper publisher and went on to the Illinois Legislature, friends organized a "bow tie" dinner in Highland and raised $10,000. In the audience were members of my old canasta club and our first family doctor. Jo Alice Pierce and I gathered the checks and forwarded them by Federal Express to our Washington office the next day.

So many vendors have been stiffed in the past by overzealous campaign managers and candidates that up-front money is needed before telephones can be installed, brochures printed, and furniture and office equipment rented. To rent even a small storefront office with the bare necessities required cash. And the growing payroll had to be met. While my modest fund-raisers did not bring in huge amounts, there were quite a few of them, and it all added up. I enjoyed meeting men and women who had been ardent Simon supporters in the past. They seemed more than ready now to raise money and join the "bow tie brigades" that were forming all over Illinois to go into Iowa.

In New Hampshire, I was disappointed at the small crowd that turned out for a Democratic rally at a widely advertised event in Hillsboro. The staffs of the six candidates (no longer the "seven dwarfs") had only each other to talk to. Why weren't more folks there? Obviously, the public wanted to meet the candidates, not their surrogates.

Rain may stop a ballgame but not a parade in Penacook, I learned, as I added another raincoat to my collection so I could ride in a convertible and wave (which I always felt silly doing). Undaunted by the rain, Mark Wagner and Ellie Fellows walked behind the car, each holding up one end of a long banner, "Simon for President." We were pleased that no other candidate or surrogate participated in the parade.

A "Beyond War" group invited me to meet at a home. It was a sympathetic audience that agreed with Paul's commitment to the Arias peace plan for Nicaragua and his plans to stop testing of nuclear weapons (if the Soviet Union kept its promise to do the same). But they were also waiting to hear more from Governor Dukakis at an upcoming debate between the governor and Paul (Senator Gore had pulled out). Arms control groups were Paul's strong allies. I told them about Paul's visits to the Soviet Union, his service on the Foreign Relations Committee in the

Senate, and his appointment as a delegate to the United Nations Special Session on Arms Control in 1978, all of which I felt were good indications of his knowledge as well as of his concern for the cause of peace. They wanted to wait a little longer before making a final commitment.

Chub and Toni Peabody insisted that I accompany them to a Greek dance near Manchester. Feeling that this might not win us any friends in a group that was very proud of its ethnic heritage and would surely support Governor Dukakis, I reluctantly joined them and had a surprisingly good time. Chub introduced me to everyone there, and they were cordial. I took pains to assure them we wanted to be a strong strong second to Governor Dukakis. I'm not fond of ouzo or retsina, but I love to watch Greek-Americans doing Zorba dances, waving handkerchiefs, and I was pulled into a circle dance.

On one of our few noncampaign days, Paul and I found the formula for a perfect Sunday afternoon: a walk around the Washington marina and over to Hains Point; pick up a pound or two of steamed shrimp; open a bottle of wine; and have a picnic while watching a Redskins football game, if the Chicago Bears were not on television. But the telephone usually intruded with campaign news or strategy that couldn't wait. With Sunday papers strewn around mingling with briefing books and xerox copies of issue papers, our small apartment looked messy but comfortable.

We never had time to read a serious book. We just barely managed to read the *New York Times, Washington Post, Time, Newsweek,* the Chicago papers and, of course, the *Des Moines Register,* the paper that everyone in Iowa reads. Paul never reads fiction, but I do, and there is nothing better suited to help pass the time in an airport waiting room or a long flight than an absorbing book. I was fortunate to find two that matched my taste: *Patriot Games* and *Presumed Innocent.* Our *New Yorker* magazines and *National Geographics* started to pile up waiting to be read on a long holiday.

Paul remained in Washington for a few days to prepare for

the Judiciary Committee hearing on Judge Bork. Lea and I headed for Louisiana where local Democrats in Lafayette plied us with Zydeco records and Cajun cooking (I'm still not sure what boudin is—but I ate it). They were infinitely more concerned with their upcoming gubernatorial election than with the nomination of the next Democratic candidate for president. A local TV talk show host who must have been watching conservative columnists Robert Novak and Patrick Buchanan too long invited me to be his guest and then started out by insulting the Democratic Party and all the candidates, including Paul Simon. Summoning up new courage, I moved to unhook my lapel microphone, and said I had better uses for my time and would leave. He apologized and we continued.

The highlight of our Louisiana trip was the press conference with Governor Edwards (famous for his motto, "Laissez le bon temps rouler"), followed by a luncheon at the Executive Mansion to meet the women agency heads and cabinet officers.

On the way to Baton Rouge, we had three near misses as the driver always turned to me when he talked. By this time, I was getting very apprehensive about new drivers and cars. Governor Edwards charmed us and took obvious pride in the appointment of qualified women in his administration. He also carefully did not endorse any presidential candidate but had high praise for Paul, mentioning Paul's well-known push for more foreign language study in our schools.

In Orlando, speaking to a convention of Missouri Synod Lutherans, I had to shift gears and talk about the meaning of the U.S. Constitution and the separation of church and state, but I managed to mention Paul several times. I suspected that the group was conservative, but for many, their pride in Paul as a Lutheran layman overcame their normal Republican persuasion. I promised to send bumper stickers and posters to all who asked for them.

Many times on the road, I felt out of touch with important campaign trends and developments, so my midnight telephone calls were expanded to include news from our press secretary,

Terry Michael, and our campaign manager, Floyd Fithian, as well as Paul. And good things were happening! Our campaign fund reached the $2 million mark at the end of September. Direct mail solicitation was beginning to produce the desired effect. More of Senator Biden's supporters joined the Simon campaign. Congresswoman Pat Schroeder of Colorado announced that she would not be a candidate for president, to our vast relief. Now the women who had been telling me that they admired Paul but were waiting to hear from Pat had their answer. Stories in *Newsweek* and the *Wall Street Journal* hinted that Paul's campaign was coming on strong and that he might well be the "sleeper" candidate.

One of the best indications of the campaign's success was the increased number of print journalists and radio and television reporters that followed Paul. Martin told me that their number was growing every day. With Paul for one day in Chicago, I saw for myself the media phenomenon. At a scheduled visit to a children's bookstore, a huge crowd greeted Paul, and an even larger group of reporters pressed in and around trying to capture a comment or emphasize a point. It was a delightful scene, and no one enjoyed it more than Paul and I! Several youngsters asked questions and received serious answers.

The event that had the most genuine expression of support was entirely unplanned and came from a well-known Dukakis supporter, former Speaker of the House Thomas "Tip" O'Neill, in Chicago for a book signing party at Kroch's and Brentano's bookstore. We dropped in unannounced and were greeted warmly by "Tip," who gave me a bear hug and an admonition to "stand by my man." With TV cameras and reporters present, "Tip" praised Paul's ten years of service in the House of Representatives and said he was well qualified for the office he sought. We understood his support for Governor Dukakis of his home state of Massachusetts, but I had a strong suspicion that "Tip" would like to endorse Paul. A picture in the *Chicago Tribune* the next day showed the obvious respect and affection the two men have for each other.

By far, the best news a candidate can receive is to hear that he is number one in a scientific poll. That was something that had eluded the Simon campaign until October 4, when we learned that Paul headed the *Boston Herald*-WBZ poll of voters in Iowa! I knew Josh King had good news when I met him at Logan Airport in Boston at 12:30 A.M. because he waited at the gate with a smile that could not be restrained. I read the story in the *Boston Herald* three times before it really took hold in my mind, and then I had to call Paul in Atlanta and woke him up to tell him. But, of course, he knew all about it before me. Anyway, it was great news to share and savor. Arriving in Manchester an hour later to stay with the Shaines, I found unbounded joy by Frances and Bob.

The next morning, I met with our New Hampshire steering committee and realized that the effect of the *Boston Herald* poll could not be underestimated. It simply breathed new life into our campaign. We felt good! I spoke at high school classes with renewed conviction and greeted the senior luncheon group with my good news. In a day full of meetings with our New Hampshire staff, there were many new aggressive field people and stops at Salem, Derry, and Concord for local media. I began to allow myself to think that we had a good possibility of being number one in Iowa and being a strong number two to Governor Dukakis in New Hampshire. The adrenalin rushed through my veins. My only sadness was that Paul and I were not together to enjoy this moment.

A gathering of students and faculty from New England College at the home of a professor and a stop at Tufts University convinced me again that student groups were eager to support Paul. An interview on WRKO in Boston was lively, and I felt more confident in facing the TV camera at WNEV, CBS in Boston, for an interview I shared with Hattie Babbitt.

Paul and I finally were together in Washington when the Democratic National Committee sponsored a debate at the Kennedy Center and a gala dinner. Paul argued at the debate that all the Democratic candidates should pull together for a Democratic victory, no matter who the candidate was. He said the candidates should quit bad-mouthing one another by saying that someone is "weak on defense," a phrase he predicted would come back to haunt us from the Republican candidate. The DNC gala was the biggest ever held—another of those enormous dinner parties where we didn't want to take time to eat but worked the crowd joyfully.

Paul headed back to Iowa, and I had a two-day respite planned for Makanda to see Sheila and Perry, wear old clothes, and walk in the woods. The newlyweds invited me to a special dinner with silver, china, and crystal gleaming on the table, as only wedding presents just out of the box can look.

Martin and I met in St. Louis where we cut the ribbon at the opening of the Simon headquarters with lots of balloons, banners, and media. We recognized that Congressman Richard Gephardt represented that district and counted on strong support from Missouri, but the St. Louis newspapers had always given Paul good coverage. The *St. Louis Post-Dispatch* had strongly endorsed Paul in every election starting with his first in 1954. There was every reason to think that we did not have to concede all the Missouri delegates to Dick Gephardt. And, best of all, our loyal supporters had raised the money for rent and equipment and were not asking the national office to finance its operation. Charles Klotzer, now a magazine publisher, was back of this move. Many years ago, he had worked for Paul at the *Troy Tribune*, his first journalistic job in the United States, after fleeing Germany by way of China.

Before Lea and I left on our northwest tour, I heard from Paul that another poll in Iowa commissioned by the Gephardt campaign showed Paul way ahead, but we could not get definite figures. When Paul called and said, "Do you have a pencil?" I knew there would be good poll figures, and it seemed that increasingly there was good news of one kind or another.

In Utah, Dave Thomas drove us to Snow College in Ephraim where a conservative student audience was polite but not like the student groups in Iowa or New Hampshire. There was a nucleus of a Simon organization in Salt Lake City, where we had a small fund-raiser and met some University of Utah students who wanted to work for Paul. Dave said his two-week vacation next year would be spent in Iowa in January working for Paul, and he would bring some friends with him. This was my second visit to Utah, and they told me that no other candidate had been out there. Maybe we had a chance to pick up the slender Utah Democratic primary vote! There is no optimist greater than a candidate's wife.

In Eugene, Oregon, Paul's birthplace and hometown for sixteen years, a friendly atmosphere greeted me as Paul's family friends rallied around with stories of Paul as a boy growing up in Eugene, where his father served as a Lutheran pastor.

In Portland, I enjoyed good press and television at different stops: a meeting of lawyers, a visit to a Safeway distribution center where disabled and retarded young people were mainstreamed into useful jobs, a Sierra Club reception, and another meeting with teachers. I was also so tired that night that I fell asleep watching television and missed my TV spots entirely.

A luncheon that started off with reservations for twenty increased to fifty and, finally, wound up with a hundred in attendance, just to hear me. I could not have been happier since there seemed to me to be a genuine interest in Paul based not on this year's campaign but on his entire progressive record in the Congress.

Our last stop was in Boise, Idaho, where, again, we met with teachers, women lawyers, and the press. All of these meetings were well attended. On a charter flight from Boise to Denver, Lea and I relaxed for the first time in four days and enjoyed a box dinner of Popeye's Chicken late that night. Meals are always a dilemma in a campaign. I'd sooner talk than eat at any breakfast, luncheon, or dinner. Fast food becomes the order of the day until you realize that a fresh green salad is what you are craving, and you'd like to try to establish a normal eating plan. I recalled Joan Mondale's exhortation to Sheila and me in 1984—we should insist on meals at the normal mealtime no matter where we were. And we were able to follow her advice for one day!

Our family reunion came faster than I planned, thanks to the need to shoot television commercials. Grandma Ruth Simon, Sheila, Perry, Martin, Paul, and I were together in Makanda for one day of nonstop television filming. The late October weather was perfect for outdoor shots, and David Axelrod's easygoing way, just letting us talk extemporaneously (no script) suited us just fine. We all wore jeans and sweaters. Paul didn't even wear his bow tie. John Jackson, a professor at SIU, made a statement for Paul, as did Ray Chancey, our Democratic County Chairman, low-key but honest and direct, based on their long friendship with Paul. *Time* Magazine photographers also took pictures during the day, and Martin was busy with his cameras.

Going back to Des Moines, I expected only one staff person to meet me at the airport but I was met, instead, by the entire staff, almost twenty people, cheering and applauding in a wonderfully happy mood. The staff size had exploded and so had the enthusiasm. Fran Sullivan, a friend from Oak Park, Illinois, and a native of Iowa, came with the group at the airport. She made the most generous offer possible—to drive me in her own car wherever I needed in Iowa and to be a full-time volunteer at the campaign office when I was in other states. She had just seen her daughter married in the fall and had taken a trip to Spain. Now she felt ready to hit the campaign trail. She knew Paul and had worked for him in his Senate race, and she had a good working idea of what a campaign day was like. We felt comfortable with each other and got along well. She came at a time when our advance staff had just started to have an impact.

Rob Johnson, a young staff person from California, told me that never again would we lose the battle of signs. If there was a candidates' forum, a Democratic function, a parade, there would be Paul Simon signs and posters in as great profusion as there were for other candidates. Paul always had advance work for his campaign swings, but my appearances had a minimum of advance. Now press releases and pictures went out a week ahead. Calls were made ahead to local Democrats. We paid return visits to county chairs and local officeholders in the courthouses.

I bought a book in Iowa City, *The WPA Guidebook to 1930's Iowa, A Federal Writers' Project,* produced in the FDR days, which gave a historical, geographical, and economic picture of Iowa towns and cities. In that way, I could refer to some local hero or recognize a family name still prominent, or make a comparison to the old days. Fran and I stopped at libraries if we had a few extra minutes and caught up with the latest magazines or wrote thank you letters there between stops.

Berkley Bedell spent a day with me in his old congressional district where he appeared to know everyone, and his former constituents came out to meet us. More and more, Iowa caucus-goers seemed willing to "commit" to Paul. A return visit to the Busy Bee Restaurant in Jefferson was a success.

More county chairs wanted to see Paul or me in their county for a dinner or rally. Our work began to show results, and we thought that coming in number one in Iowa just might happen! With Sheila and Perry now residing in Des Moines in a new and larger apartment, Des Moines was almost as much home as Makanda. They brought a TV and radio, a popcorn maker, and a coffeemaker with them from Illinois. They put up maps, cartoons, and pictures on the walls. Until February 8, 1988, we had a home in Iowa.

The New Hampshire campaign staff wanted me to join Paul in their long-planned "Octoberfest," a helicopter blitz of several cities with a kickoff rally at Notre Dame College in Manchester. My flight to Boston was delayed, and after an over-the-speed-limit ride to Manchester, I arrived to see a crowd of about five-hundred in the college gym, cheering, clapping, and clearly in a buoyant mood. Students had Paul Simon T-shirts on, everyone was waving signs, and Paul was just ascending the stage. I was urged to join him and pressed my way to the front. Paul spoke and thanked everyone. I told the throng that good things were happening in Iowa, and the whole place exploded in cheers and applause. We stayed to shake everyone's hands and then went to the bowling alley. There is something about seeing a candidate for the presidency rolling a ball down an alley that conveys a common man image. The press gets a picture of the candidate that is different, and not too much harm is done if he doesn't get a good score. The press corps at this event was the largest we had ever seen, reporters from *Time* and *Newsweek* magazines, *U.S. News & World Report,* the *Los Angeles Times,* and "Good Morning, America," among others.

In the next three days we covered a good piece of New England in a helicopter. The Kennedy School in Cambridge was our first stop. I was terrified initially to be in this four-seater glass bubble, but after a while I enjoyed the view of autumn foliage and the skyline of Boston. We flew over the Seabrook Nuclear Power Plant on the coast of New Hampshire and saw only too clearly that an evacuation of the area in the event of an accident would be difficult at best. When the fog was too heavy to go to Berlin on the northern tip of the state, we rented cars and continued our journey. Overall, we showed a power play designed to capture attention, and it succeeded. It was also fun to be with Martin and Paul. What wasn't fun: returning to Washington in a small charter plane buffeted by rain and high winds, but I survived that too.

Pam Huey had scheduled more interviews in Washington with *Women's Wear Daily* and *Time* magazine, while Paul reviewed briefing books in preparation for debates on the environment and domestic issues. Another poll showing Paul clearly number one in Iowa added to our upbeat mood. A CBS poll gave him 20 percent. In six months he had come from 1 percent, with little or no chance given him by the media, to the number one place in Iowa. It was no time to relax, but we voted ourselves a night off to celebrate the tortoise catching up with the hares.

1. Shortly after Paul announced his candidacy, even the simplest things like looking at the lake from our deck in Makanda, became a "photo-opportunity."

Photography by Martin H. Simon

2. Frequently our home in Makanda became a TV studio, as in this run-through for the David Frost series, "Road to the White House."

3. Averaging three to four radio interviews a day, I became quite at home in the studio.

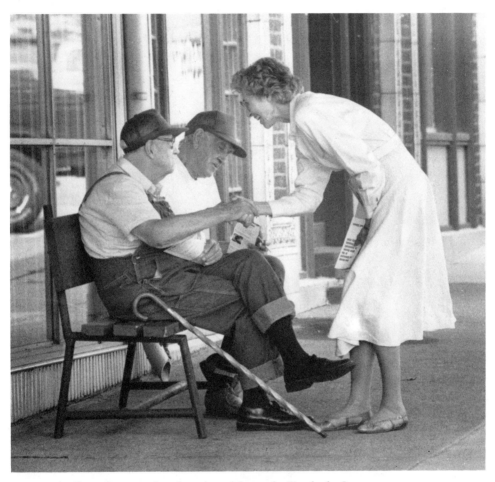

4. Greeting a pair of senior citizens in Keokuk, Iowa.

5. Paul alone in a motel room. We called each other every night to share the good news—or disappointments—of our days on the road.

6. Paying attention to "Notch-Babies" in Iowa.

7. Despite dropping temperatures, our spirits ran high as we neared the big day in Iowa.

8. Caucus day in Des Moines: the eyes of the world were on Iowa and Paul.

9. Even with flowers from Dan Rather, our second-place standing didn't blossom into first.

10. With the Republicans capturing the headlines on February 9, smiles were still easy to come by as we set out for New Hampshire aboard the "Bow Tie Express."

11. Hard to believe, but not everyone was impressed with Paul's campaign style.

12. A warm welcome at the Democratic Convention in Atlanta.

Our lives, and those of our children, were enriched by working for the nomination. We strived as a team for a goal that turned out to be unobtainable, but we gained a knowledge of the needs of Americans that we will never forget.

★ 8 ★

Emotional Roller Coaster

While the Senate staff and the campaign staff differed sometimes as to the best use of Paul's time—each group claiming priority—debate preparation brought the two groups together in a constructive way. In one day in our small apartment in Washington we had two groups come in for a discussion. The first group heard Paul Maslin, Paul's pollster, discuss the implications of his latest poll for the remainder of the Iowa and New Hampshire campaigns. The campaign staff, Paul, and I learned that the Maslin poll confirmed the CBS national poll showing Paul in the lead and Dukakis very close. It also showed strengths and weaknesses. We were all well aware that Governor Dukakis had the Massachusetts advantage in New Hampshire and much more to spend on staff, TV, and other things. These were sobering thoughts, but there was an upbeat mood that seemed to say, "We can do it!"

The campaign staff stayed to listen to the Senate staff talk about environmental issues for a New Hampshire debate and domestic issues for a debate in New Orleans, back-to-back. As I looked at the group, some sitting on the floor enjoying the give-and-take as questions and answers were tossed around, I had the feeling that this seemed more like a college class with its favorite professor. I listened, kept them supplied with Pepsi and coffee, and answered the phone. The importance of debate prep became more of a problem as the number of debates for Democratic candidates grew every day, with more and more groups wanting to see and hear the candidates respond to their particular concerns.

There were never enough political stories in the newspapers, as I eagerly scanned the *Washington Post* and *New York Times* each morning on the few days we were in Washington. The thump at the door that announced the early arrival of our newspapers usually woke me up. I fixed a cup of coffee while Paul still slept, and looked for columns and news items that told us how the various campaigns were doing so I could give Paul some favorable comment. Every morning we were together one of us would ask the other, depending on who read the papers first, "Anything in the papers?" which meant, "Is there anything about Paul Simon on the campaign in the papers?" The political columnists observing Paul's rise in the polls began to mention him with more frequency.

I picked up *Newsweek* on a plane in early November 1987 and read the George Will essay on the back page that said, in effect, that the Republican candidates were dull and yearned for the excitement that Paul Simon was providing the Democrats. "Simon dispenses the 90-proof New Deal-Fair Deal whiskey—Democratic fun." I had to restrain myself from nudging my seatmate on the plane and saying, "That's my husband he's writing about." A column in the *National Journal* by Jack Germond and Jules Witcover said, "Paul Simon may turn out to be the big surprise." Reason told me that writers like to hedge their bets, and they had to take notice of Paul even if early on they had downplayed his chances for the nomination.

On a foray into New Hampshire I had the fun of traveling with Nina Solarz, the wife of New York Congressman Steve Solarz. Nina volunteered to be with me for two days for coffee parties, press interviews, and TV in Exeter, Nashua, Plymouth, Laconia, and Meredith. We met as wives of the members of the Ninety-fourth Congress who were elected in 1974. We had traded visits to each other's congressional districts, ours in rural

Southern Illinois where Steve and Nina met farmers and coal miners and saw soybeans, wheat, and corn in the fields. This stood in contrast to their district in Brooklyn that we visited—crowded, urban, a new home for many refugees from the Soviet Union. Steve and Nina had enthusiastically endorsed Paul in April and were pulling together a Simon for President organization in New York.

One of the best evenings in the entire campaign was at the country home of Mary and Steve Algren in New Hampshire. After dinner with their young family, a group of their activist friends joined us around a roaring fire for a good discussion of all the issues: arms control, environment, education, acid rain, the trade deficit, and the Seabrook Nuclear power plant. Their concern for their children's future and how that future would be directly affected by the next administration was obvious, and so was their interest in Paul's candidacy. Nina and I agreed that the evening succeeded in every way as we took names and addresses of those who wanted to volunteer time for Paul.

Nina also called my attention to the way my red suit looked. It looked too big. I had lost about fifteen pounds at this point and it showed. I almost lost my gold wedding band in the shower one morning when it simply slid off my finger and I scrambled to get it in the drain. I promised to eat more and Nina saw to it that I did!

The staff asked me to represent Paul at the Florida State Democratic Convention since Paul was scheduled to be at Colby College in Maine to receive an Elijah Lovejoy award at a writers' conference. Paul's first book was a biography of Elijah Lovejoy, an abolitionist and the first U.S. martyr to freedom of the press. A mob in Alton, Illinois, killed Lovejoy in 1837, for writing antislavery stories in his paper. I knew Paul would enjoy the occasion in Maine. I wasn't too sure how I would enjoy the Florida trip.

I traveled alone this time and my apprehension grew because we had only a nucleus of an organization in Miami. The meeting at the Fontainbleu turned out to be a pleasant surprise.

Although Governor Dukakis and Jesse Jackson were there, each with a numerous staff and supporters, signs, banners, and posters, a good number of Floridians came to hear me speak for Paul before the main dinner. Many of those in the room had supported Paul in his Senate race and were delighted that he defeated Charles Percy. After giving three TV interviews and working the crowd in the big ballroom, I felt Paul Simon had a good chance—if we could get a campaign staff, a headquarters, and some funds in Florida. All the candidates acknowledged Florida's importance on Super Tuesday, March 8, when a group of Southern states would hold their primaries. I wished that Paul could be there. Representative Claude Pepper, the venerable Congressman from Miami, saw to it that they introduced me from the podium, and Governor Bill Clinton of Arkansas mentioned my name in his opening remarks to the large crowd. I had a long day and an exciting one. I could not get to sleep that night pondering our chances and hopes in Florida.

Our staff in Iowa had long been promoting the biggest Democratic event of the year in Iowa—the annual Jefferson-Jackson Day Dinner on November 7 in Des Moines. I've been to those large "JJ" dinners in Chicago, Washington, and New York, and I assumed that this would be one more of the same—lots of people, buzz, and excitement, but little attention to the speakers or the program. Was I wrong! Each Simon congressional district coordinator, every college Simon organization, and all of our far-flung volunteers had been working to have a huge Simon delegation at the dinner, either on the floor of the Armory or in the galleries. Long before the dinner started, in fact from the moment I arrived in Des Moines, I could feel the atmosphere supercharged for Paul. Busloads of our friends came from Illinois—the "Bow Tie Brigades"—vans and cars brought students from Southern Illinois University, the University of Illinois, and the University of Wisconsin, to join our student followers from Iowa campuses. I caught up with Paul at a press conference. Barry Surman, the Iowa press secretary, whispered to me, "He's hitting homers." Terry Michael, the national press secretary, said, "He's so good with his answers, I'm crying!" Sheila, Martin, Perry, and I joined Paul on the podium as he concluded, and I got a big kiss and a hug from a very happy Paul. The *New York Times* quoted Paul the day before that he saw more of the other five candidates than he did of me.

Leading a parade to Veterans' Auditorium in the late afternoon with hundreds of students in back of us carrying banners and signs and chanting "We love Paul," I had never felt so excited in any campaign. The sight of twenty or more TV and still photographers walking backwards in front of us as we surged forward is etched in my memory as a spectacular sight. This is the real joy of a campaign—to be together, to feel confident that you have a chance to succeed, and to be buoyed by people who believe in you. We had a perfect fall afternoon in every respect.

Someone miraculously appeared with my suitcase and the green dress that I planned to wear to the dinner. I hastily changed in an RV in the parking lot of the Vets' Auditorium (I would have preferred a shower and a few quiet minutes) and joined Paul and the other candidates and wives in the green room. I noted that Kitty Dukakis and Jackie Jackson were the only absentees. Tipper and Al Gore, Jane and Dick Gephardt, Hattie and Bruce Babbitt, and Paul and I mixed and mingled with Mike Dukakis and Jesse Jackson, each wondering, I am sure, how the evening would be viewed by the media and the political correspondents. We could hear the roar of about 8,000 people gathered in the hall and discerned cheers and yells for all the candidates. Waiting nervously to be introduced, I imagined that this might be what it is like to be in an Olympic event or on a football team, waiting for the kickoff; or like the Christian martyrs being led into the Coliseum—maybe a combination of all three. We heard Bonnie Campbell introduce all the Iowa officeholders, state and national. They took their seats on one side of the podium.

Then we lined up—Paul and I were first—and heard Bonnie

saying "Here is the next president of the United States!" With that, Paul and I walked in to the most overwhelming roar of cheers, yells, and applause that we have ever heard. And since we were first, it sounded extra good!

We looked out on the floor from our raised dais and saw huge bow-tie banners, and then many, many bow ties floated down from the galleries on little parachutes. I looked around and sighted Sheila and Perry at a table on the floor waving to us, and Martin nearby with his camera on a monopod. Finally, all the candidates were introduced, we took our seats, and tried to eat a bite of dinner. It was impossible, and we didn't care. Throughout the dinner the galleries engaged in organized chants. We responded to each one for Paul by standing up, waving our napkins, and trying to say thank you. I recalled the Polk County steak fry early in April when we had no staff, no one to cheer for Paul, and we were 1 percent in the polls. What a difference a few months of solid campaigning and field work made!

Each candidate had ten minutes. Paul carefully timed his speech to meet that requirement and had practiced with a teleprompter. He was ready. Before the presidential candidates had their time, however, there were lengthy filmed interviews on a big screen of all the Democratic state officeholders. Senator Harkin spoke from the podium. It was late in the evening when Paul finally addressed the throng. This time it was better to be the first speaker. (Usually it is best to be last.) I joined him for a minute and waved. Paul was firm in his delivery, in good voice, in charge, and the audience interrupted him repeatedly with cheers. David Axelrod filmed the speech, and we used parts of it for a TV commercial later. A superb floor demonstration followed that we relished, again standing and waving as Simon people marched past the podium. The other candidates took much longer than their allotted ten minutes, and each one had a floor demonstration. So we could not leave until 11:30 P.M. At 2 A.M. we were still awake, too excited to sleep, while Martin joined the staff to celebrate.

Reading the *Des Moines Register* early the next morning at the airport, I noted that only one picture appeared from the JJ dinner—Paul and I waving to the crowd! The story featured the revelation that Bruce Babbitt and Al Gore admitted to smoking pot in their youth. I remembered again the Polk County affair when all the candidates except Paul had their pictures in the *Des Moines Register* the next day.

I slept from Des Moines to Chicago and from Chicago to Detroit. Lea and I flew to Ann Arbor where I spoke at a student rally for Paul. A former intern of Paul's and two young women students organized a Simon group on campus and had a good, although not large, audience. I proudly accepted a University of Michigan sweat shirt from them. Another talk followed to a group concerned with the plight of Soviet Jews. I talked about Peace Links and the Congressional Wives for Soviet Jewry and told them about Paul's work to seek the release of Naum Meiman, an eminent physicist still detained in Moscow on flimsy excuses, and that Paul had been successful in bringing several Russian Jews out of the Soviet Union. The group knew what Paul had done, and they wanted to help him.

After three weeks on the road, living out of a suitcase, staying in different hotels, motels, or private homes every night, enduring cold showers or scalding hot ones, I rejoiced at the chance for a reunion with Paul in Chicago; to shop for a winter coat and boots, and to have a few hours alone. Paul and I headed for our favorite spot for Dungeness crab on the near north side and walked a mile or so after dinner, responding to cheerful greetings along the way. Michigan Avenue was getting ready for Christmas with tiny twinkling lights in the trees and glorious shop windows to look at. Shopping for Christmas presents would not be possible, we agreed. (All we wanted: an endorsement from the *Des Moines Register* and to be number one in the Iowa caucuses, and one of those did come long after Christmas.)

We would be home in Makanda for Thanksgiving and for Christmas. To be together with Sheila, Martin, and Perry for a few days would be the best present we could give to each other. Bill and Sheila Hurley took me to a football game at Notre Dame, his alma mater, where we had a good time watching Notre Dame beat the "Crimson Tide" of Alabama. I enjoyed yelling and cheering and for a little while forgetting about presidential politics.

But only for a bit. Pam Huey and I met at Midway Airport in Chicago the next day and flew to Madison, Wisconsin, for a meeting with county chairs, held a press conference at the state capitol, and had good receptions there and in Milwaukee. University of Wisconsin students in Madison who had traveled to the JJ dinner in Des Moines were there to greet me with the huge bow tie banner they carried all around in the Des Moines floor demonstration. Their faculty leader and professor, Midge Miller, told me that they came on a school bus and slept in sleeping bags on the floor of our Des Moines headquarters. They loved every minute of it, they assured me. They even planned to go back to Iowa before the caucuses and work in the precincts again.

On my way back to Iowa a fellow passenger recognized me from a picture in *USA Today,* which featured a story on our family and had a small picture of me, in color, on the front page. Even after all our months of campaigning, it still surprised me to see my picture in any paper.

Stops at Wartburg and Coe Colleges featured small but encouraging audiences, and the University of Northern Iowa got out a good group of students and professors for Paul. Fran Sullivan, Elinor Bedell, and I spent some time in Berkley Bedell's old congressional district, where we were the recipients of some extraordinary hospitality. Bonnie and John Bogen in Emmetsburg waited up for us to arrive late one evening, and then fixed a big bacon and egg breakfast for us the next morning before our first early meeting at a bakery. In Paulina we met the Wilsons who gave us a place to rest in the late afternoon and a splendid dinner before we went to a meeting at the local library. There seemed to be a much greater interest in Paul at these stops, triggered in part by Paul's status as front-runner in the polls and, I hoped, by Paul's message, still concentrating on arms control, slowing down our defense spending, helping the underclass, putting more funds into education, working towards a peaceful settlement in Central America, and long-term care for the elderly.

I was frequently asked if Paul was a "liberal," sometimes in tones that seemed to equate "liberal" with "radical." I asked these folks to make their own judgment based on his record: concern with civil rights and human rights and improving social programs, such as Social Security, Medicare, Head Start, college-loan programs, and better health care, among others. Paul is conservative in fiscal matters since he favors a constitutional amendment to balance the budget and believes that the president should have a properly drafted line-item veto. He looked for practical answers to everyday problems, I said; labels did not make any difference when it came to solving those problems. The "L-word" was a favorite epithet for our Republican friends to hurl at us, but I hoped that Democrats would understand the difference.

Before we could head home to Makanda for Thanksgiving, I made one more trip to New Hampshire. On the way I met a lawyer from Salinas, Kansas, on the plane who recognized me and said he wanted to help our campaign. We traded cards and I made another convert. The mood in New Hampshire was as good as ever. A *Boston Globe* story about a new poll aided that feeling. The headline said "Dukakis Slipping—Paul Simon Gaining."

Our stop in Dartmouth where only seven women came to a meeting to discuss issues of concern to women with the usual predictable questions (i.e., Equal Rights Amendment, pay equity, Title IX) was a disappointment. We made the obligatory stop at Dixville Notch, obligatory since the entire population of thirty-four registered voters—nineteen Republicans, six Democrats, nine Independents—is the first precinct in New Hampshire (indeed in the country) to vote and usually reports its vote at 12:10 A.M. on primary and election day. But we had a long drive to meet eight Republicans and two Democrats. All the inhabitants work at a resort hotel called the "Balsalms." I doubt that we changed any minds. I would have enjoyed being a guest at the Balsalms though.

In Berlin, New Hampshire, we had some desultory drop-ins arranged by our staff person, including a sing-along at a senior center, and a cribbage tournament at the VFW. Bob Shaine saved the day, or rather the evening, by buying a drink for the men at the VFW. Some days were not as good as other days, I concluded. This did not turn out to be a great day.

To add to my discomfort, I read a story in the *Washington Post* indicating a growing doubt that Paul's calls for a balanced budget and a jobs program were consistent. Talking to Paul on the phone that evening, I detected concern in his voice. But he said that the front-runner status would bring more scrutiny to everything he proposed, and we should expect more of the same.

Bad weather delayed my flight out of Logan Airport, but I finally met Martin in St. Louis where we hoped to rendezvous with Paul, Sheila, and Perry and drive home for Thanksgiving. Alas, they were stranded by the same bad weather in Kansas City, and their flight was canceled. Tired and hungry, Martin and I rented a red Cadillac (the only car left at the rental agency) and drove home to Makanda in great style, stopping only for a quick McDonald's along the way.

Whirlwind grocery shopping was called for. On the day before Thanksgiving, I made two pies, and Grandma Simon brought along lots of bakery goods from Collinsville to help feed the hungry crew. We all started to relax with rental movies and popcorn when we learned of the sudden death of Mayor Washington in Chicago. Both phones rang constantly after that with reporters asking for comments by Paul on what this would mean for Chicago and for his campaign. We made arrangements to attend the funeral and scaled down our plans for a birthday party/fund-raiser for Paul set for the same day in Chicago.

On Friday we entertained the press for one hour at our home, making a big splash on local television that evening. The *Southern Illinoisan* ran a color photo of Paul in our living room with a "hometown boy makes good" story by Tim Landis. A year ago at Thanksgiving we had all but ruled out the presidential bid. This year Paul led in the *Des Moines Register* poll and was starting to close the gap in New Hampshire with Governor Dukakis.

Over the weekend Paul and Martin made a quick tour of Oklahoma, Florida, and Kentucky before they arrived in Chicago where I joined them. The city of Chicago was in mourning. Every municipal office had closed. We saw men and women weeping as they stood in line to walk through City Hall and view the body of the late Mayor. The funeral service the next day was almost impossible to reach by car—the crowds were so enormous—and Martin, Paul, and I finally made it to the "national dignitaries" section and listened to the tributes (Governor Thompson spoke and left) and thrilled to the music of the massed choirs. Our fund-raising dinner and birthday party for Paul was subdued but a great success nevertheless. Our finance board was encouraged by yet another national poll, CBS/*New York Times*, with Paul Simon number two after Jesse Jackson, but only 1 percent ahead of Governor Dukakis.

Early the next morning I left to make a luncheon speech in Davenport, Iowa, and returned the same day to Washington to be with Sheila, Martin, and Perry in the audience for the Kennedy Center nationally televised debate with the six Democratic candidates. The events of the previous week had not left much time for debate preparation, but it seemed obvious that Paul Simon would be attacked by one or more candidates on reconciling his jobs bill with his plan to balance the budget. Paul had no problem explaining it, but it took some time. The debate rules specified a one-minute answer, which was definitely not enough time. I arrived just in time for the debate and was not at the debate preparation, which Lesley Stahl was allowed to watch with a CBS camera crew.

From the beginning of the program I felt uncomfortable. The seating arrangement for the families on the stage allowed us to see only the backs of the candidates. I would have preferred to sit in the audience and see their faces as they responded. Tom Brokaw walked around like a prosecuting attorney firing questions and expecting quick answers. He also managed to stand in front of Paul much of the time whenever he paused, thereby blocking him out from the camera. The candidates were permitted to ask questions of each other. It did not take Dick Gephardt long to attack Paul for what he called "Reaganomics with a bow tie." In the debate preparation, I learned later, Paul and his staff agreed that since this question could not be answered in one minute, he should say he had in preparation a white paper with all the details. This was not a strong reply, and I realized that he appeared to be ducking the question, an unusual gambit for Paul. In other areas he did well. No one starred in this debate.

One of our senior campaign staffers followed us back to our apartment and bluntly told Paul that he should take a ten-day time out for meditation, insist on better debate prep, leave more time for reading, and study of the issues. He was quite adamant about it. The idea of a ten-day holiday at this juncture was laughable and out of the question. But we understood that for the next debate coming up in New York there would have to be more rest time before the event, and any debate prep would henceforth exclude TV reporters. The presence of outsiders at a give-and-take session had to be inhibiting at best, and it prevented the participants from feeling free to comment. It disturbed me to learn later that Ms. Stahl criticized Paul's performance in the debate and thought his debate prep was inadequate! In one column we read that Governor Dukakis was always given three to four hours "quiet time" before a debate, which *had* to help his performance.

The next day the *Des Moines Register* reported that Paul lost ground in the debate but did well with Republicans and that Dick Gephardt received a strong negative rating for his attack on Paul Simon. Any setback at this point would be critical and I felt uneasy. Our campaign had been going well, but now Paul was getting criticism for making a serious proposal to balance the budget and eliminate the deficit in three years—and asking Congress for additional taxes if that did not work. The other candidates, with the exception of Bruce Babbitt, were either avoiding the issue of the budget or making feeble attempts to deal with it.

As always seems to happen, the depression of the Kennedy Center debate and its aftermath was partially obliterated by a good event. This time it was our invitation to dinner at the home of Joan and Jim Gannon, the editor of the *Des Moines Register*. I had attended a *Des Moines Register* editorial board meeting earlier, where Paul handled questions on just about every possible topic. I wanted to meet Mr. Gannon and form my own impression of this man who might just possibly be a deciding factor in the Iowa caucuses if he chose to lend his weight in an endorsement for Paul Simon. He seemed fair, I concluded. We enjoyed our evening with them. When I complimented Joan on the salmon, asparagus, and wild rice, she admitted that she had a special chef in for the evening. If Paul was being considered as the recipient of the prestigious *Des Moines Register* endorsement at this dinner party, I thought all had gone well.

When an opportunity to go to Texas for a few days came along, Pam Huey and I jumped at it. I welcomed a change from Iowa and New Hampshire. Jim and Connie Calaway, active in the Democratic Victory Fund and careful not to make any public endorsement at this early date, were our hosts in Houston. Their penthouse was the most extraordinary home I have been in, with a pool on the roof and a skyline view of Houston. On the curving balustrade to the second floor, Native American art works were arranged. We had some frank talk

about the Kennedy Center debate. Both Jim and Connie expressed disappointment in Paul's handling of the balanced budget question and urged a more thorough study of the whole
question. It was constructive criticism.

The main reason for our Texas visit was to participate in a
forum in Cleburne where Governor Dukakis, Senator Gore,
Hattie Babbitt, and I would be on the firing line. On the way I
greeted a group of Simon people in Houston, put in an appearance in Austin at a luncheon for Democratic women
(where Gore and Dukakis spoke but the sponsors did not allow
me to speak for Paul), and attended a reception for me at the
state capitol.

Jim Hightower, the ebullient Texas Agriculture Commis-
sioner, served as moderator. Before the debate started, I joined
in working out details on the order of appearance and the use
of microphone at either the table or the podium. The Dukakis
handlers insisted that *all* the speakers sit at a table and use the
microphone while seated. I said that they could do that if they
wished, but I preferred to speak from the podium; that as a
lawyer I felt better about speaking when standing up. In a
behind-stage debate, I opposed six Dukakis staffers. Nevertheless, I would not concede. The matter was resolved when we
learned that the microphone would work only from the
podium. Were they sensitive about the governor's height? The
abrasive nature of the Dukakis staff irritated me.

Governor Dukakis, who knew nothing of this little drama,
greeted me warmly when the forum started. Hattie Babbitt
made a short address for her husband and left. I remained to
answer questions with Senator Gore and Governor Dukakis. It
was another late evening before we returned to Dallas. There
seemed almost no point in going to bed at 2 A.M. only to get up
at 5 for the early flight to Washington, but Pam and I managed
to do that.

The flight from Dallas to Washington was unusual in that the
entire passenger list consisted of a Jewish delegation planning
to join the march of 200,000 from the Ellipse at the White

House to the Capitol to urge freedom for Soviet Jews. I in-
tended to do that also. Pam and I were folded into the warm,
happy group who passed out cookies and candy and sang songs
during the flight. Paul had to be in Cambridge to participate in
an hour-long, nationally televised interview with Marvin Kalb
from Harvard's Kennedy School of Government.

A camera crew from CBS "Sunday Morning" followed me as
I met members of our Illinois delegation on the Ellipse. Cling-
ing to Congressman Steve Solarz in the crush of thousands of
people, I made my way to the dais that seemed to have a heavy
Republican overload—Morris Abram, chairman of the National
Conference on Soviet Jewry, Vice President George Bush, Senator Bob Dole, and Congressman Jack Kemp, among others.
The wonderful strong feeling of participating in this march
made the adrenaline flow, although my feet were icy cold on
this blustery, chilly day. My introduction by Morris Abram as
Paul's wife brought cheers from the crowd.

Later that afternoon Bob Pierpoint of CBS interviewed me
for "Sunday Morning." Paul's appearance on the Marvin Kalb
show—a one-on-one interview with questions from students
and faculty at the Kennedy School—was a marked improve-
ment over the Brokaw debate, the staff told me, and I suddenly
felt a lot better. Later that week, Paul also did well at the
Governor Cuomo Forum in New York. I joined his lengthy
debate prep and saw to it that he had a good rest. It made a
difference. Debates took a lot of time away from campaigning
in Iowa and New Hampshire. While we hated to say no to a
debate opportunity, we also wondered whether it was a case of
diminishing returns, as the answers to the questions by all the
participants were becoming more and more predictable and
programmed, and with less spontaneity.

The Iowa staff grew insistent that I return to Iowa and laid
on a heavy schedule for me. This time Fran Sullivan and I were
joined for a day by David Lauter of the *Los Angeles Times* and
Ginger Davis, a journalist and community activist. A foursome
like this could be uncomfortable on a long trip, but Ginger and

Dave proved to be excellent travelers, eager to see the campaign from the viewpoint of the candidate's wife. The weather threatened in early December, and I hoped that I wouldn't need the snow boots I left in Washington. In Parnell, Iowa, I recalled my Irish background to a group of Irish Democrats and had a good time.

Later in the car, Ginger said "You're real!" Dave was writing all the time and kept talking to people. We had an overflow crowd at a reception in Iowa City, always a stronghold for Paul, and went from there to Cedar Rapids where I spoke at an Iowa Peace Institute Forum. For the first and only time in the entire campaign, I was joined by Jackie Jackson. No other candidate's wives were present. Given only a few minutes to speak, I talked about Paul Simon and his UN experience, his support for the INF Treaty, and my Peace Links work. Jackie said she had met a lot of world leaders and her contribution to world peace was to raise five good kids. I had to admit that she beat me by three in that category. We posed for pictures together. In Dubuque I spoke to United Auto Workers retirees and a high school audience, neither one of which seemed overly happy to greet me.

Hearing on our car radio dire predictions of a bad winter storm, Fran and I returned to Cedar Rapids for the night as the snow started to come down in earnest. Our plans to drive to Des Moines for a luncheon the following day were put on hold the next morning when we heard the TV weathermen urging everyone not to drive unless it was a matter of great necessity. The thought of staying in Cedar Rapids for another day made us reassess the situation. With some assurance that the interstate would be better, we started out. Fran is a careful driver, and the journey called for all her skill. Many cars and trucks were abandoned by the side of the road or in the median. Snow plows were working, but the blizzard covered the highway in a matter of minutes. I thought about my snow boots in Washington.

We made the long journey to Des Moines and reached our headquarters about 11 A.M. Assuming that we would be congratulated on this feat, I was surprised not to see anyone in the office. Fran and I called out "hellos" and no one answered. We found the entire staff crowded into Pat Mitchell's office. We watched with them as Gary Hart announced on TV that he was reentering the presidential race.

This had to be the most bizarre news of the eight-month campaign! After all the bad publicity, the jokes and cartoons, and public humiliation that the Hart family had been through, how could Gary Hart think that he could still be a believable candidate? More important to us, what would this do to Paul's front-runner status? Paul tried to be reassuring when I talked to him late that evening, but I knew as well as he that there might be problems for us. Now Paul and all the candidates would have to comment on the Hart campaign once more. We did not welcome Gary Hart's resurrection. I went through the motions of reassuring the Democrats at our luncheon meeting that Hart's reentrance was an ego trip, and he would self-destruct a second time.

I wanted to believe that very much as I prepared for a trip with Lea to Arkansas, Georgia, and Florida.

★9★

Down To The Wire in Iowa

I was counting the days to Christmas like a child, but I tried to concentrate all my attention on our Southern swing through Arkansas, Georgia, and Florida. A tight schedule allowed us in one day to meet Governor Clinton in Little Rock in his office, address an adult literacy group, talk with Daisy Bates, editor of a black newspaper, make a case for Paul Simon to a group of students at Catholic Boys' High School, and be on local TV at a fund-raiser/headquarters opening. After I spoke at the high school, Father Tribou, the principal, said I had converted him from being a "male chauvinist," and I would be a great asset in the White House. Very high praise, indeed.

John Starr, the editor of the *Arkansas Democrat* in Little Rock, was a real grouch, and we wasted our time with him. He wrote:

> I decided on the day Hart filed in the New Hampshire primary that I would henceforth refer to the Democratic field as Captain Sleaze and the Six Space Cadets. When Jeanne Simon, wife of candidate Paul Simon, visited my office during her recent trip to our state, I told her about my nickname for her husband and his fellow contenders.
>
> Mrs. Simon was not amused. Instead of laughing, she reached into her purse and pulled out a cartoon that had run in the *Des Moines Register* on the morning after the resurrected Hart filed as a candidate in the New Hampshire primary.

The cartoon showed Hart as a seventh dwarf, one called
Sleazy. It was published on the *Register*'s front page.

Before dawn the next morning, we were on our way to
Atlanta where I met with Democratic Party officials planning
the July convention. I allowed myself to dream of being there
with Paul Simon giving his acceptance speech to the cheering
throngs, but then I returned to the reality of our campaign. At
a luncheon meeting with Jean Young, wife of Atlanta Mayor
Andrew Young, and three black women leaders at the Ritz
Carlton, I strongly suspected support among three of them for
Jesse Jackson and only a polite interest in Paul Simon. The chief
executive officer of DeKalb (pronounced "DeKab") County—a
Democrat—stressed his Lebanese background and then pro-
ceeded to give a long harangue on how he thought Paul Simon
was mismanaging his campaign. I had no opportunity for dialogue with him, and I was glad to get this unpleasant but
necessary exercise over.

A 6 A.M. flight the next day took us to Miami where a delightful woman, Rose Ruban, whom I had met at the Florida
State Convention, held a coffee party for me with a reporter
from the *Miami Herald* and local TV present. A large sign
greeted us in her condo: "Welcome Jeanne Simon."

My happiest memory of the Southern trip comes from Orlando where I attended a Hanukkah dinner and was invited to
speak from the pulpit by Rabbi Larry Halpern at the Congregation of Liberal Judaism Temple. Speaking from the pulpit
is a formidable challenge. I tried to center my message on the
successful march for Soviet Jewry on December 6, the Congressional Wives for Soviet Jewry trip to Vienna, and Paul's efforts
to get Naum Meiman out of the Soviet Union. The congregation gave me a warm response, and I felt great relief not
to have fumbled such an opportunity.

As we headed back to Washington I realized that I was actually looking forward to a day of cleaning, doing laundry, going
through the mail, even cooking. With these simple tasks, I can

see positive results: a stack of folded towels and underwear, a pot of spaghetti sauce, empty wastebaskets, and a clean, fresh smell in our apartment. A one-time cleaning woman left me a note saying she would let me know when she could return, but I never heard from her again.

Martin and Paul were in New York for Paul's appearance on "Saturday Night Live" with singer Paul Simon. Paul had received an offer earlier to be on this popular TV show, in a skit which we thought would have poked fun at Senators Hart and Biden. He declined. Tonight the two Paul Simons were to walk in at the beginning of the program, each claiming to be the emcee.

My Paul Simon is not a stand-up comedian, and I feared that he might in some way look silly and hurt himself. My fears were quickly dissipated as the exchange of banter went well for both Pauls. Paul and Martin called a few minutes after his appearance to get my reaction. "First rate," was my assessment. Paul's appearance on the David Brinkley Sunday morning talk show the following day seemed dull by comparison. "Saturday Night Live" reached tens of millions of people, a real coup for Paul. Subsequent repeats of that program during the writers' strike increased Paul's recognition factor. Paul received $676 for the Saturday Night Live appearance and similar amounts every time it appeared after that, which we did not expect.

Our last big event before the Christmas holiday was the opening of the Boston headquarters for Paul, an outdoor event with about 2,500 people in a huge rally in downtown Boston. For the first time I wished there were a little more protection for a candidate and his family as Martin and I saw Paul swept up in the crowd and felt ourselves being propelled in another direction. It was all very friendly and exciting, but also a trifle scary.

Paul's mother slipped and fell on ice and was in a nursing home, unable to join us for Christmas as she always has done. Sheila and Perry had the Christmas tree up and decorated and a fire going in our fireplace when we arrived two days before Christmas. With glorious freedom for a few days, we walked in the woods, played canasta and Trivial Pursuit, and watched movies until the early hours of the morning. After candlelight services at Our Saviour Lutheran Church and midnight Mass at St. Francis Xavier, our friends wished Paul well, and many commented on his appearance on "Saturday Night Live."

The holiday ended on December 26, when we held an all-day staff meeting at our home to review old TV commercials and consider new ones, finalize the white paper on balanced budget and debt reduction, and plan for the next six weeks in Iowa and New Hampshire. Gary Hart, whose reappearance had cut Paul's lead in the polls by almost half, cast a shadow over the discussion, although our polls continued to show Paul doing well. We were not as confident as we had been a few weeks ago; there was tension and uncertainty. We knew only that we had to do better.

Paul and I headed south for a brief campaign tour in Florida—Daytona Beach, Palm Beach, Clearwater, and Tallahassee in two days. We accepted the offer of Gwen and Jerry Berlin to stay at their home in Miami Beach for a few days, an offer that included the use of their car. It was far from being a carefree holiday as Federal Express envelopes arrived regularly with issue papers, and the phone rang constantly. Paul retired to the study to type out statements. I caught up again with thank-you letters and organized a mass of speech material, notes, scraps of paper with names and messages I could hardly read, and threw out old speech notes and clippings.

We cheerfully passed up invitations for New Year's Eve parties and went to a movie instead. We had never been to a bowl game, but as two die-hard football fans, we eagerly joined the crowd on New Year's Day to watch the University of Miami and the University of Oklahoma play in the Orange Bowl, thanks to a friend from the University of Oklahoma who sent us tickets. Paul proved to be, even without his bow tie, a great attraction for the fans around us who asked for autographs on the programs, took pictures, and pledged their support. A UPI photographer was also on hand for a picture.

The first of the year brought a new look to Paul's entourage. The Secret Service moved into the picture, although Paul had at first dismissed the idea of their protection. But we met with three agents and they told us there had been threats on his life and strongly advised their presence. The possibility of preventing harm to Paul outweighed any lessening of Paul's outgoing, handshaking style of campaigning. I was happy to have their help. Agent John Parker said he and the agents on this detail would study Paul's style and try to accommodate their protection to him. Paul's code name was "Scarlett." They made it clear that their job was to protect Paul but assured us that they would also keep an eye on me, Sheila, Martin, and Perry when we were with Paul. Their professional demeanor reassured me. Paul, as he always does, quickly learned about the agents' families and backgrounds and made friends with all the men and women who were to be with him twenty-four hours a day until the end of his campaign. When Paul was in our apartment in Washington, an agent stayed at the door night and day. The agent standing watch at the door changed every half hour. On the floor at his feet was a small attache case that held an automatic rifle.

Our home in Makanda is in the country, far away from neighbors and difficult to locate.

"Surely the agents don't need to be there," I said. With a straight face, Agent Parker told me they had already surveyed our home and the surrounding fields and forests, which offered untold hiding places.

"A Winnebago Wagon will be on your property as a command post whenever Paul is there. Agents will monitor visitors and circle your home at night," he said. Although I felt that I was in a TV mini-series, I acknowledged that they knew more about the need for protection and how to go about it than I and did not offer any more suggestions. I received an "SS" pin to wear which allowed me to pass their checkpoints.

"Why did they want to know your coat size?" I asked Paul when they left. "For a bullet-proof coat they may require me to wear on occasion," he replied. I shuddered at the thought.

After the holidays, Pam and I left for North Dakota where the temperature in Fargo reached zero. We planned a two-day tour of North Dakota and Minnesota. The warmth of the greeting at the airport led by Senator Quentin Burdick and his wife, Jocelyn, made me forget the chill. Both the Senator and Jocelyn joined in my introduction as the TV cameras and reporters crowded around. Once again, I was happy to have the support that only someone else who has been through the same experience can offer. The Burdicks had been in many campaigns and knew it was tough to be on the move in strange places, meeting strangers, looking for support.

Ham Thompson, our Minnesota campaign coordinator, hired a small, poorly heated charter plane, but it did have two pilots and two engines. In spite of the bitter cold, our events went well until we reached St. Cloud. At a meeting at St. Cloud State, students wearing suits, carrying briefcases, and sporting large Dole buttons showed up to needle me about Paul's stand on Nicaragua and aid to the Contras. I noticed Pam exchange a worried glance with Ham when I answered one more question about Gary Hart.

"Should Hart's extra-marital conduct be considered a factor in his quest for the nomination?" a reporter asked. "If he takes a bimbo to Bimini, I believe voters have the option to weigh that with everything else," I replied.

Ham got up from the back of the room and walked over to Pam. "Is Jeanne getting tired?" he asked. Pam worried that this candid comment would make national news.

After that drubbing, we were invited to what I thought would be a friendly reception at a nearby home. Instead, the host seemed irritated by our invasion, refused to turn on any lights except in the kitchen, parsimoniously doled out coffee in styrofoam cups, and talked about what was wrong with the Democratic Party. I couldn't wait to leave. On the way to the airport, a supporter told me that this phenomenon was known as the "Stearns County" syndrome—i.e., a success anywhere else will fail in Stearns County.

In Isanti, Minnesota, 120 eighth-grade students awaited my arrival for a "teach-in." Signs and banners of welcome were everywhere. The principal greeted me and escorted me to the assembly hall. I spoke about the political process of nominating a president, what the two political parties stood for, and talked about each of the candidates, Republican and Democratic, before I said why I believed Paul Simon to be the preferred candidate. I hoped that these students would carry the message home to Mom and Dad that evening.

That night Pam and I had pizza and wine in our rooms at the Minnesota Club in St. Paul and thawed out. Martin and Paul called from Birmingham, Alabama, to tell me that only Senator Gore and Paul were in a debate that evening and that it was a success for Paul. More than that, he reported that a CBS/*New York Times* poll had good news:

% All Dems in Iowa		% Dems Who Will Attend Caucus	
Hart	25	Simon	24
Simon	18	Dukakis	16
Dukakis	11	Gephardt	13
Gephardt	10	Hart	13
		Jackson	11
		Babbitt	7
		Gore	1

I was in a jubilant mood when I met with the teachers at a convention of the Minnesota Education Association in Minneapolis to talk about Paul. Not only did I address the group, but I received a standing ovation when I finished. Teachers in every state I visited knew about Paul's record, and as a group they were politically active. I believed Paul had a solid base with teachers in Minnesota.

We made another trip to New Hampshire where bad weather again greeted us, but interest was really picking up. Pam and I stayed in private homes where the guest rooms looked inviting, but lacked heat. One morning my fingers were so stiff and cold that I could hardly button my blouse. There were more days of being up early and getting to bed late and not much to eat, but February 8 was less than a month away, I kept telling myself.

The *Des Moines Register* holds a debate every four years for candidates of each party—an affair that is considered highly prestigious. In addition, it is seen all over Iowa. This debate had an added interest—Senator Hart—and journalists speculated as to how he would perform. We feared that he might dominate the whole performance, but Paul had plenty of time for debate prep and felt comfortable.

After a light supper of clam chowder and salad, we all left with the Secret Service for Vets' Auditorium. As soon as Paul opened the door of our apartment, six Secret Service agents surrounded him and escorted him to the car. Paul and I followed a lead car of Secret Service agents and listened to the agent in our car talking about "Scarlett's" arrival. The agent at the site gave the number of meeters and greeters waiting for Paul. We learned not to open the car door but wait for the slap on the side of the car, an "all clear" signal, after which the doors were opened. Again, Paul was surrounded by agents in a wedge and led to the holding room before the debate. They didn't try to stop him as he reached out to clasp hands with all the friends waiting for him. They moved with him and sometimes gave a shove or two to get through. Impassive to the cheers and yelling, they functioned as they were taught, to keep looking for the odd person and not to let anyone get too close for too long a time. It was unusual for us, but we understood what they were doing and why.

The debate went well. Paul gave good, concise, clear answers. He was in a relaxed mood. Our fears about Gary Hart proved empty. He had nothing new to contribute and certainly made no waves.

By this time I felt like a commuter on the early Northwest flight from Des Moines to Chicago. Even the flight attendants recognized me. At a stop in Chicago to speak to a coalition of arms control groups, the choice for endorsement was between Jesse Jackson and Paul Simon. We gave a ride to the Jackson spokesperson from the airport to the event in downtown Chicago. It became a contest between surrogates, and Paul Simon received the endorsement.

A bumpy charter flight to Carbondale from Chicago took so long that I had no time to change my dress before we went to a fund-raiser that was the largest ever held in Southern Illinois. These hometown people had no doubt that Paul Simon would win the Iowa caucuses and go on to win the nomination. In back of the podium on the stage was a replica of the rear end of a train, the "Simon Special," reminiscent of Harry Truman's whistle-stop express. As the speaking program started, the Secret Service agents stood on each side of the stage looking out at the audience. At one point a balloon popped causing an agent to reach for his gun and giving the audience a good demonstration of his quick response.

We could not linger long in Illinois. John West, a former governor of South Carolina and the head of Paul's organization in that state, invited Lea and me to a two-day tour of Charleston, Columbia, and Greenville. Paul and I had met Lois and John West years ago when John and Paul were lieutenant governors in their respective states. At a meeting of the nation's lieutenant governors, the Wests and Simons found common ground. We were proud to be invited to be a part of John's inauguration as Governor of South Carolina in 1970. I met with local Democrats, spoke at a college, and enjoyed a sight-seeing tour of old Charleston with Waring Howe, our local coordinator. We opened a Simon headquarters in Columbia with a lot of TV and press.

Our flight from Greenville to Washington was detoured to

Savannah, then to Atlanta, and we finally arrived at 2 A.M. exhausted. After the South Carolina trip I managed to go through the motions of holding a meeting with staff at our campaign headquarters, answering letters, and shopping for groceries on a rare day off. I literally crawled into bed at 6 P.M.

The next morning I knew that I could not possibly make the trip to Minnesota for a series of media interviews, even though this would make some people unhappy. I had a temperature of 101; I was coughing, sneezing, had aches and pains and dizziness, all the symptoms of the flu. Looking back on the last two weeks of nonstop campaigning, mostly in cold weather, little sleep, and odd meals eaten quickly, I could understand that I might not have much resistance to a virus, but this was the wrong time to be sick! When I talked to Paul in Iowa, he made me promise to stay in bed and drink hot red wine with lemon juice, his guaranteed cure for colds and flu. For three days I drank orange juice, swallowed cold pills and cough medicine, and worried about Paul's drop in the polls. Dick Gephardt now ran ahead of Paul in every Iowa poll and was getting stronger, based in part on some very effective "protectionist" TV commercials. I wanted to be with Paul, Martin, Sheila, and Perry so we could take comfort in being together and cheer each other a bit.

I joined the campaign again in Ames, Iowa, to attend a debate on farm issues. Returning once more to Iowa where the temperature hovered at 17 degrees, I was still sneezing and coughing and full of apprehension, not knowing which way our campaign was headed. My only consolation was to reflect on the volatility of campaigns and to hope for better news soon. At least I would be with Paul for a few days.

A strong clique for Dick Gephardt with the farm groups was visible at the Ames debate. The staff urged Paul to confront Dick with his inconsistent farm votes, and he did, but not in an "attack" manner. Paul never enjoyed being a "hatchet man," yet in the 1984 Senate race when Senator Charles Percy tried to tie Paul to the Ayatollah Khomeini, he mounted a strong counterattack. I sat with Sheila and Perry at the debate and felt better just to be with them. Sheila told me of her exchange with Bruce Babbitt at a Democratic fund-raiser in South Dakota where she spoke for Paul. Bruce complimented her on her presentation and told her she had improved as a speaker. She told him, "So have you!"

Yet another debate was scheduled for New Hampshire. After deicing the wings on our charter plane and fixing the frozen landing gear, Paul and I made the long trip to Portsmouth, New Hampshire, for the debate where John Chancellor served as moderator. My sister-in-law, Sheila Hurley, joined us there. We watched as Chancellor irritated Senator Hart in his introduction of the candidates, alluding to his romantic liaisons. Paul had good answers for Chancellor, but from his position at the end of the row had a hard time getting Chancellor's attention to comment and ask questions. Two days later the candidates held another debate, this time in Boston's Faneuil Hall. Walking to the hall we saw the kind of campaign picture that makes such a good "visual" for the evening news: snow falling, lots of cameras and flashing lights, and a screaming crowd of young people behind barriers with Simon signs, yelling "We want Paul." Lots of hands were reaching out to Paul. Many Secret Service agents were watching the crowds. Inside the hall, Sheila Hurley and I had front-row seats to see Marvin Kalb question the assembled candidates. Again there were no surprises.

A long-awaited opportunity for Paul and me to appear together on the NBC "Today" show came in Boston. Early in the morning, we drove to a local NBC studio and were within fifteen minutes of air time with ear microphones in place when Agent Tim Scanlon quietly announced that there was a fire in the building. We walked down the nine flights of stairs and drove away in the Secret Service car as the fire engines pulled up. Within five or six minutes we learned that fire fighters had the fire under control, and it was just possible we might make it back to the studio on time. We ran up the stairs where the smell of smoke lingered in the air, put the microphones on again, and then calmly greeted Jane Pauley for a five-minute interview.

More requests for interviews came in, and I responded gladly. CBS selected four candidates' wives, two from each party, for a Lesley Stahl "special." Hattie Babbitt, Elise DuPont, Elizabeth Dole, and I—all lawyers—were interviewed separately. A reporter from *People* magazine stayed so long that Pam Huey suggested "Jeanne's voice needs a rest," and showed her to the door. With the help of May Mineta, my friends at the Woman's National Democratic Club, many of them Congressional Wives and all of them devoted Democrats, held a luncheon/fund-raiser for me in Washington with TV coverage.

Our friends and supporters in Maryland asked me to make some campaign stops in Bethesda, Frederick, and Baltimore. A reporter from the *Baltimore Sun*, Susan Baer, spent the day with Pam and me. Carol Greenwald, a member of Paul's campaign finance committee, lent us her comfortable Buick for the day, and it turned out to be a good day in all respects until we reached downtown Baltimore around five in the evening when the car suddenly lost power at an intersection. The local mechanics could not determine what was wrong. The host at our next reception, State Delegate Gerald Curran dispatched his sons to pick us up, and we continued with our appointed rounds. Ms. Baer wrote:

> The car is dead. Totally dead. No lights. No brakes. A battery as kaput as Joe Biden's shot at the presidency. Is it just our imagination or has the lovely pink and blue twilight just faded to black? Is it just our imagination or is there a lot more ice on the ground in Baltimore than there was in Washington?
>
> It's cold. It's dark. Jeanne Simon is a day out of bed with the flu and the borrowed Buick Skylark she's been traveling in all day has just decided, in the middle of York Road on the tail end of rush hour that, thank you very much, I've had enough.
>
> But the wife of presidential candidate Paul Simon has not.

She still has miles to go before she sleeps on this non-stop adventure that's called the campaign trail, and nothing, not the flu she's been tending with Vicks cough drops and tissues, not even a broken-down Buick, is going to slow her down.

By this time in the campaign I had become accustomed to the unexpected happening. I also realized the terrific impact an appearance on national television has. People, even strangers on planes, recognized me and said "I saw you on TV." A man on one flight said he would save a 25-cent stamp and wrote out a check for $100 and gave it to me. The Brennan family from Boston recognized me at Logan Airport and told me they were excited about my Irish background. As I waited for my baggage at LaGuardia, I noticed a woman whisper to her husband who turned around and stared at me. Recognition was wonderful, but not when I had to listen to a long explanation of someone's notion of how to improve our foreign policy posture or some esoteric topic. Paul and I were on the cover of *North Shore Magazine*, sold in the North Shore suburbs of Chicago. Martin took the picture and it turned out to be the best of the campaign. *Newsweek* magazine used pictures by Martin in a feature story on Paul. Now when I saw Paul on TV, I looked for Martin walking backwards in front of him, along with the cameramen and photographers of the working press.

Lea, Patty Montgomery, and I drove to Richmond, Virginia, on January 30 to attend a big Democratic dinner where Senator Gore and I spoke. Addressing a dinner audience of over 1,200 might have bothered me a few months ago, but by now I had only minor butterflies. The Democrats in Virginia leaned heavily to Senator Gore rather than Paul, but I gave it my best shot telling them that Paul was campaigning in Iowa, the first test of presidential popularity, not bypassing it. Senator Gore had abandoned Iowa and now concentrated almost solely on southern states.

Arriving back in Washington long past midnight, and weary,

I was in bed when the phone rang. Martin, in Iowa with Paul, said, "Would you like some good news? Dad wants to talk to you." Paul could hardly contain the excitement in his voice. He had received the editorial endorsement of the *Des Moines Register!* Just when our campaign needed a boost, one week from the Iowa caucuses, this was the best possible news, no matter where he stood in the polls. I tried to get Sheila and Perry on the phone, but they were not home. I learned later they had heard about the endorsement at 9 P.M. and headed promptly for the Hotel Savery where they could "spin" with reporters, staff people from other campaigns, and celebrate. The entire Iowa staff was celebrating that night! The endorsement was a statement of the merit of each candidate, but for Paul there were comparisons to FDR and Harry Truman, and even Abraham Lincoln. It could not have been better. In part, the *Register* said:

> Of the Democratic contenders, we believe Simon has the makings of the best president.
>
> That conclusion is based partly on his long and unwavering record—a record capsulized in his one-liner: "I'm not a neo anything; I'm a Democrat." What the record shows is a man who has decent instincts and who sticks by them.
>
> Now, as he runs for president, Simon's lifelong interests match the needs of the times. He offers the correct diagnosis: The United States has diverted too much of its resources into the military rivalry with the Soviet Union while Japan and Western Europe, less burdened by military expenditures, forge ahead in the economic rivalry.
>
> He calls for shifting resources to education, jobs, the environment, peace—not a novel program but one offered by a candidate whose record shows unquestioned commitment to it.
>
> Once before in troubled times the nation turned to an unpretentious man from downstate Illinois. The times are not quite as troubled now, and perhaps the man is not as great, but he is good, honest and eager to turn the energies of government toward long-neglected needs.
>
> Paul Simon would be the best nominee for the Democratic Party.

The next morning I called my brother Bill and my cousin Marie with the good news. Sheila Hurley said she couldn't understand why it took so long to see the Lincoln comparison. Going into the final week of the Iowa campaign, every candidate had been hoping for this—and Paul had it! I couldn't wait to join him for the final round of campaign rallies.

★10★

No. 2 in Iowa,
No. 3 in New Hampshire

In spite of a lingering cough and still fighting fatigue, I felt exhilarated with a new dedication to win the Iowa caucuses. Before I could join Paul and Martin, a Hadassah group in New Hampshire asked me to meet them and answer questions about Paul's views on Israel and the Soviet Union.

Andrea Durkin, a Tufts University senior who took off a semester to help Paul, met me at Logan Airport. We drove to Nashua, stopping first to meet with members of Paul's executive committee. They were all delighted with the *Des Moines Register* endorsement, but they wanted hard-hitting television spots using that endorsement. Paul made it clear early in the campaign that he did not want negative ads. The question only Paul could answer was: was it negative to use the *Des Moines Register* endorsement that said Gephardt was the most disappointing of all the candidates because of the way he pandered to many special interest groups, and to call attention to his flip-flops on many major issues.

The twenty-five or more Hadassah women who crowded the living room were friendly. I could not help but wonder why Governor Dukakis was not their obvious choice since Kitty is Jewish. They assured me they were probing the backgrounds and experience of the candidates in foreign affairs, especially with reference to Israel and the Soviet Union, but they also cared about civil rights, and were concerned about the possibility of mandated prayer in the public schools. Kitty's religion was indeed a factor, but only one, they made clear.

When I talked to Paul late that evening he was still in an upbeat mood although Dick Gephardt was ahead in the polls, and yes, he said, we would be putting together tough radio spots for Iowa, but not negative ones.

Paul was holding forth at a senior center in Sioux City Iowa, surrounded by press, and Secret Service agents, when I arrived. Martin told me how the whole atmosphere of our campaign had changed—it was supercharged with new drive and energy. At subsequent stops in Cherokee and Le Mars I felt the excitement as Paul entered the room. There clearly was a difference in the audience reaction, as well as Paul's attitude. A rally at the Star-Lite Motel in Fort Dodge was superb! The crowd cheered, bands played and balloons drifted through the air. Our advance team made sure all the elements of a successful rally were there, and we loved it. What made this rally particularly poignant for me was my recollection of a meeting I held there in September, shortly after Senator Biden's withdrawal. That group was small—a Sister from a Catholic school with two students who took notes for a class assignment, the county Democratic chairperson, Ken Motl, and three Democrats with many questions about a balanced budget and the federal deficit. They were "leaning," but not ready to commit to Paul. Now I saw them, not only committed, but cheering at the top of their lungs!

The mood change was obvious on the charter plane as we flew to Cedar Rapids—the staff was light-hearted, singing the Waterloo Rotary's special song for Paul—"B O W T I E, that spells Bow-o-tie." We all joined in—even Paul. A reporter from the *Los Angeles Times* asked Paul why he was so "pumped up." Paul said the crowd enthusiasm at Fort Dodge did it.

Paul Maslin gave us the latest polling results, which were mainly good. The *Des Moines Register* endorsement had been a significant factor, and there was clear movement for Paul. However, a Boston TV poll and the last *Des Moines Register* poll projected Dick Gephardt the winner.

Late that night, we ordered a pepperoni and onion pizza and huddled with David Axelrod and Paul Maslin over the game plan for the next few days. David played the tapes of the proposed radio spots—they were an honest account of the voting records of Paul and Dick Gephardt. There was nothing negative about them. Would they be considered negative? I wondered. Most definitely, yes, by the Gephardt staff. Our job would be to turn off any interpretation that tended to be negative. The poll said Paul looked like an underdog, coming on strong at the end of the long campaign. This posture was encouraging to our staff and volunteers, and brought many more friends and students across the Illinois border into Iowa to aid the cause.

Lea and I detoured for two days to Rapid City and Pierre, South Dakota. On the way back to Des Moines we planned a stop in Lyon County, the only county in Iowa that Paul or I had not visited. Paul wanted to say that our campaign was in every one of Iowa's ninety-nine counties.

Rapid City is not Midwest. It is West and beautiful, surrounded by the Black Hills. Two radio interviews, and a visit to the *Rapid City Journal* went well, and after a brief lunch stop at the home of Cynthia and Kurt Ireland, we were on our way to a teachers' meeting, and a reception at a Democratic forum. Dinner at the Alex Johnson Hotel looked great but I passed it up to talk to a dozen hard-core supporters. The temperature in Pierre was 6 below zero when we arrived at a lonely airport late in the evening. The temperature in Lea's motel room was also chilly. She piled on every coat, sweater, and blanket she could find to keep warm, while I was comfortable in another room.

Norma Brick-Samuelson planned a busy day of visits with legislators at the state capitol, a stop at a senior center, radio interviews, and a visit to the state library (a big "Welcome Jeanne Simon" sign was over the door), and a luncheon at the Elks Club.

I had just finished speaking to an AFL-CIO convention in Pierre when Patty called to say there had been a schedule change. I had to pick up Paul's schedule, she said, since he was called back to the Senate to vote on a Contra aid bill. The schedule now included two events in Minneapolis after the stop in Lyon County. Worst of all, I wouldn't catch up with Paul, Sheila, Martin, and Perry for another day.

A note on our schedule for the Lyon County stop read: "There are very few Democrats here and you probably won't be able to help PS at all." How true that was! In Rock Rapids, Lyon County, six Democrats turned out at 4 P.M. Lea and I did not spend much time there but hurried back to our cold charter plane for the flight to Minneapolis.

Two fund-raisers were scheduled for Paul and now I had to explain that he was in Washington. The enthusiastic crowds understood, so I relaxed and together with Joan Growe, Minnesota Secretary of State, met everyone there, including several state legislators, Democratic Farm Labor people who still hold the memory of Hubert Humphrey sacred, and a former intern of Paul's, State Senator John Marty. I recounted the illustrious records of Hubert Humphrey and Walter Mondale and urged the Minnesota Democrats to consider Paul in the same tradition, a Democrat concerned with the welfare of working men and women, a Midwesterner with the common touch, and with a proven track record of winning in a tough year in a big state. Paul called late to tell me he would be giving the response to President Reagan's weekly radio address, another break. He was still number two, but gaining, he added.

Our family reunited in Council Bluffs. To our surprise we had a family night scheduled and nothing changed it. A tired and happy crew had dinner at a Chinese restaurant, with Secret Service agents nearby. We relaxed and exchanged war stories of the past few weeks until we were laughing so hard we were crying. For the ride to our motel, the escort police from Council Bluffs put Sheila and Perry in the back seat of their car with the metal grill in the middle, and no door handles. Martin got a great picture of the two peering out the back window.

Time was running out, but our scheduled events were not. The advance team planned rallies at Briar Cliff College in Sioux City, Coe College in Cedar Rapids, and Cornell College in Mount Vernon. At each we met friends and volunteers from Illinois who were spending the weekend in Iowa before the caucuses, making personal calls and visits to people who had indicated they were with Paul or were "leaning."

My fatigue vanished as each event reached new heights of fervor. Our family cheered for Paul as lustily as the rest, enjoying the crowds that clearly were "pumped up." We could not predict victory, but at each stop, the party leader in charge waxed more eloquent and the audiences responded in kind.

Returning to our apartment in Des Moines late that evening, Paul reviewed possible topics for discussion on the David Brinkley's ABC Sunday morning program to be aired from Des Moines. George Bush would be on for the Republicans. We expected Paul would be asked about the campaign's financial situation, and the latest estimate of his standing.

At midnight, Martin told me that Dan Rather was coming for coffee early Sunday morning. I set the alarm for 6 A.M., got up and did what I could to make our apartment look a little more orderly, and brewed some strong coffee. After all that effort, we learned that he was not coming and that we would meet him later that afternoon.

A TV crew filmed Paul at church and then it was time for David Brinkley, George Will, and Sam Donaldson. Before the program started, we chatted with Barbara and George Bush who appeared relaxed although the Vice President had not been endorsed by the *Des Moines Register* and was running behind Senator Dole in all the polls. The *Des Moines Register*'s final story before the caucus said that Gephardt was ahead by a slight margin, but added that Paul had the momentum and a firm base of support. Paul also received the endorsement of the *Quad City Times*, another boost to our hopes.

Working until the last minute in the final forty-eight hours involved a flying trip to Cedar Rapids for a pancake breakfast put on by the local Democrats. Governor Dukakis and Kitty were there making the rounds when we arrived. We chatted briefly with them. Dick Gephardt and Bruce Babbitt were also expected.

Back in Des Moines, Paul answered questions on a C-SPAN call-in program, and we met Dan Rather for coffee. He was interested in background, Paul's status in the polls, and how it had shifted when Gary Hart returned to the field. All the TV anchormen and women were looking for some new bit of information, some angle that could distinguish their story from the others. Perhaps Mr. Rather sent flowers to all the wives of candidates—I don't know—but he sent me flowers on the night of the caucuses that greatly helped the decor of our rooms at the old Fort Des Moines Hotel, and lifted my spirits as well.

A rally Sunday afternoon at the Savery Hotel was the biggest, noisiest, most exuberant of all. Bill and Sheila Hurley and Marie and Tom McDermott spent the last two days in Iowa making calls, nailing down "iffy" voters, and answering last minute questions. Now I could see them cheering. The crowd in the Savery ballroom provided the group dynamics that only an allout rally can give. I looked out at the audience and identified people that I had seen many times in the past ten months—staff, volunteers, students, peace people, teachers, union members—and thought how much we owed them for their commitment.

Snow was falling on the last day of the Iowa campaign. We had no way of judging what that would mean to the expected turnout. Snow and cold weather are a part of the Iowa scene in February, and most folks would not consider that an obstacle if they really cared about a candidate.

Paul, Martin and I, two Secret Service agents, and two staff people were in one plane, the press in another as we started off for the final round. In Davenport we went door-to-door in Mayor Hart's neighborhood, and followed that with similar stops in Cedar Rapids, Des Moines, Council Bluffs, and Sergeant Bluff. My red coat and red hat showed up well against the white snow; my boots were warm, and we were having fun.

In Des Moines, we drove to a neighborhood that had been selected by Pat Mitchell for a good "visual," but we were acutely disappointed to see only a few camera crews at the first home. After a brief chat with the residents, we walked out to the sidewalk and then, over a small hill, we saw a wave of journalists and cameramen, puffing with exertion, trying to catch up. The streets were plowed but it was still rough going as we trudged along, trying to accommodate all the press.

The most unique interview for me was with a Soviet camera crew. They appeared amused and puzzled at the same time at the whole scene and particularly wondered why I was along.

"I enjoy campaigning, and I want to help my husband win the nomination—this is the American way," I explained and added "spasibo" (thank you) in the spirit of glasnost.

The closer we came to the end of the day, the more our spirits soared. At every stop we picked up little tidbits of information to further fuel our hopes. We heard that Governor Dukakis was going to ask his supporters to go for Paul on the second round, if Dukakis was not viable on the first round. The chairman of the notch babies endorsed Paul. Bob Squier, a well-known political consultant, said on the "Today" show that he thought Paul would win. Someone told us that Dick Gephardt had been totally inaccessible to the press for two days—and that was hard to believe. Before we could land at noon in Des Moines, we had to circle for a few minutes. Our pilot announced: "Vice President Bush's plane is taking off for New Hampshire." We wondered why he was leaving so soon—before the caucuses had even started.

At 4:30 P.M. in Sergeant Bluff, it was "wheels up" for the last trip in the Iowa campaign, and on to Des Moines to await the outcome of the caucuses. Unlike a state with a primary where the candidates wait for the polls to close and hope for early returns an hour or so later, we had to wait for the caucuses to start—and they could go on for a long time. Our family and our campaign manager nervously watched television, answered the telephone, and fended off requests for interviews.

Terry Michael arranged for groups of TV camera crews and still photographers to take pictures from 7:30 to 8:30 of Paul watching TV, and our family trying to look as though this happened to us every day. We did remember the night of the Senate victory in 1984 when we followed much the same scenario, and hoped for the same happy result.

Early good news from Des Moines and Iowa City was diminished by late results from farm and rural areas where Dick Gephardt managed to capture the lead. In a rush to be on the ten o'clock news, the Iowa Democratic Party declared Dick the winner of the presidential preference poll and the delegates as well, before all the caucuses had reported in. The National Election Service (NES) count stopped with only 70 percent of the precincts reporting. That night we did not know the count was incomplete. It was no landslide, but we realized that Paul had lost, and with that loss we deemed the nomination was lost as well.

The hardest part of the evening was not trying to be cheerful with family and friends but to descend to the ballroom floor and greet the crowds that had come to proclaim victory for Paul. Never mind that Paul and I had participated in countless elections, and that we always said to each other on election day—"We can lose this one—let's be ready"—it still takes courage to acknowledge defeat gracefully and thank the people who believed so strongly in their candidate. Martin, Sheila, Perry, and I followed Paul, accompanied by Secret Service, through labyrinthine halls and back elevators to reach the ballroom. For a minute it looked as though he had won!

The packed ballroom echoed with cheers for Paul, and shouts of "On to New Hampshire" as we made our way to the microphones. It wasn't over, I kept saying to myself. We'll work harder, and New Hampshire has a primary, not a caucus.

We had only a few hours of sleep that night before we settled down to the grinding task of beginning again in New Hampshire. Paul was up at 4:45 A.M. to be on the "Today" show, "Good Morning America," and the "CBS Morning Show." The

"Bow Tie Express" left Des Moines at 9 A.M. bound for New Hampshire with friends, supporters, and media aboard. In retrospect, we should have been ready, as Governor Dukakis was, with an upbeat statement. Governor Dukakis hailed his dismal third place in Iowa as "winning the bronze medal." We should have, at least, claimed credit for winning the silver.

More cold weather and snow greeted us in Manchester, New Hampshire, where campaign director Mike Marshall assembled his entire staff, supplemented with many volunteers who had come on their own, to greet our arrival. Our spirits lifted and it wasn't long before Bob Shaine, Mike Marshall, and an energetic young lawyer, Dan Callaghan, revived our hopes for a strong number two showing in New Hampshire.

Initially, Dick Gephardt got some help from his "Iowa bounce" and polls showed Paul in third place behind Dukakis and Gephardt. But in a few days, with the help of hard-hitting TV and radio ads, the tracking polls of the *Boston Globe*, ABC and CBS began to show movement for Paul. The ads stressed the difference between Gephardt's votes in Congress and Candidate Gephardt's rhetoric. Ralph Nader issued a press release calling attention to Gephardt's shift to a quasi-Republican stance on a number of issues. The *Washington Post* ran an editorial on the same theme.

Paul is an optimist and we took new heart from every little scrap of positive information for our side. Paul and I split up again so we could cover more ground. Sheila and Perry struck out in one direction. Paul and Martin, with press and Secret Service agents, went in another.

By a happy accident, Sheila and Perry were scheduled to be at the Robert Frost Motel in Derry the same night I was. I crunched through the snow to get to their room where they had socks drying on a radiator and were having a picnic of Pepsi, potato chips, and popcorn. We had a great time together.

Late that night a knock on the door of my room awoke me. The owner of the motel received a phone call from Paul, and since there was no telephone in my room, he put on boots and a parka to tell me Paul had called. He said he had told Paul that I was "tucked in for the night." The next day the paper in Derry outdid even his hospitality—Paul received their editorial endorsement!

With Andrea Durkin driving a van, Lea and I put in long days in New Hampshire. I talked to high school classes, stopped at libraries, and campaigned the streets of little towns. There is nothing so satisfying as meeting a stranger and asking for a vote for Paul and getting a hearty, positive response. But I'll have to admit there is nothing quite so devastating as being told where to go with my campaign folders!

Andrea Durkin's driving skills and knowledge of New Hampshire geography were put to the test as we sought out voters in remote corners of the state. Late for a dinner meeting one evening, Pam Huey, Andrea, and I became lost out in the lonely country.

Backing up on an icy road to change course, the van got stuck in the snow, and we heard that awful sound of wheels spinning. With great skill, Andrea somehow pulled the van out, and then drove to a spooky-looking farmhouse to ask for directions. With only a full moon lighting the way, Andrea trudged through the snow to the door. She returned to let us know that not only were we very close to the right home, but that the couple at this house was also going to the meeting.

Kathy and Chuck Mitchell welcomed our late arrival with hot cider and a houseful of teachers who were eager to hear more about Paul. That night we were guests of Ed Nelson, a former missionary to China, whose rural home and hospitality were exceptional. And the bedrooms were warm!

A kind scheduler granted me a one-day furlough to return to Washington, which I gratefully accepted. On my catch-up day doing laundry and going through the mail and papers, Paul called three times, excited and happy. Al Haig withdrew from the Republican race, and since he had referred to Paul as "the guy with a dead bat under his chin," I had no sympathy for "I'm in Charge Here" Al. Sheila and Perry called me to say they were celebrating their five-month anniversary at the Sheraton Tara in Nashua, enjoying room service and just signing the tab since their funds were at an all-time low. I encouraged them to "live it up."

On Valentine's Day, urged on by Terry Michael, our press secretary, and mindful of the flock of photographers that were our constant companions, Paul gave me a dozen red roses. Since his sentiment rarely is given to such extravagant displays, I dismissed the flowers, but cherished the card that read: "Love Today and Always, Your Paul."

The two days before the primary were full of rallies, meetings, photo opportunities, and press interviews. All the rallies featured large crowds, and at each Paul called for questions at the end of his remarks so there was every opportunity to disagree, comment, or praise the candidate. Usually there was some of each category.

The forum I recall fondly was held at the Sisters of Mercy Convent in Manchester, at the invitation of a volunteer, Sister Susan Caldwell, whose endorsement and organizational skills we highly prized. I was amused to watch the Secret Service agents stand near Paul in the Convent parlor, their eyes moving around the room, scouting out those wimpled nuns, trusting no one. Recalling my days at Catholic schools, I almost found myself saying "thank-you Reverend Mother," with a curtsey, as we left.

Early in the morning on February 16, Paul and I greeted voters at several polling places. At one, we ran into the Reverend Pat Robertson, whose stock had risen with his surprise number two showing in the Iowa caucuses. Suddenly, it struck me as being very funny that Pat Robertson, the televangelist who claimed his intervention with the Almighty had caused a hurricane to change course, was considered a serious candidate for our nation's highest office. I caught his eye, we laughed together, and he hugged me for the benefit of a waiting photographer. The picture of the two of us caught in this embrace is not one of my favorites.

While Paul held TV and radio interviews, Sheila, Perry, Lea, Andrea, and I moved around to more polling places, getting as close as we could to influence the voters.

Rumors abounded during the day as to Paul's fluctuating chances for coming in number two. When Chris Wallace from NBC-TV came over to our luncheon table and whispered that he had heard Paul was showing surprising strength in exit polls, I wanted to cheer. The long, exhausting week from the Iowa caucuses to the New Hampshire primary finally ended when the polls closed and we gathered at the Shaines' home for a buffet supper. Our enjoyment of their hospitality was brief, for early returns showed Paul in third place. As expected, Governor Dukakis was first, but unexpectedly Dick Gephardt ran second. Paul ran well in college towns, but lost the blue collar vote in Manchester and other urban areas.

If Iowa was depressing, this news had to be lethal to our campaign. To add to our chagrin, the platform we all crowded onto to hear Paul suddenly collapsed, miraculously hurting no one. Paul claimed the platform he ran on was a lot sturdier than the one he stood on!

When I couldn't find Sheila later, Martin told me he saw her crying, and I knew that I felt the same. We had allowed our hopes to ignore reality, and now it was time to make some difficult choices.

★ 11 ★

No. 1 in Illinois

Decisions made in haste often miss the big picture. There was too little time to plan a course of action for Minnesota and South Dakota and not enough money to carry it out. A dozen of the brain trust gathered in our room at the Sheraton Tara late on the night of February 16 to figure out the next move. Do we quit now? Do we go on to Minnesota and South Dakota? If we do go ahead, can we pull together the necessary funds? I had no desire to continue, but I was in the minority.

Our decision, after talking it over at length: hold a press conference the next morning and announce that if Paul did not come in first in either Minnesota or South Dakota he would withdraw. Terry Michael suggested that Paul frankly admit that the campaign funds were low, and ask folks to "call Paul" with pledges of support. Sheila, Perry, and I left for Washington, dispirited and exhausted, assuming the campaign was virtually over. We talked about going home to Makanda. Sheila hoped to return to the Legal Assistance Office in Carbondale. Perry wanted to finish his Master's thesis at SIU. His topic was: "Interest Groups and the Iowa Caucus"—the observations and experiences he gained in the Iowa campaign qualifying him as an expert in this field. I was prepared to go to Minneapolis, but I was not looking forward to it.

Late that evening, Martin called with the astonishing news

that phone calls from all over the country were urging Paul to stay in the race. People were promising checks and volunteering help. Martin said this unexpected response had completely changed the mood and our plans for the next assault on the primaries. Our friends in Illinois, in particular, insisted that Paul stay, as a favorite son if need be, but also to give the delegates pledged to him an opportunity to go to the Democratic National Convention. My mood changed immediately. I was very happy that it wasn't all over, and now I looked forward to Minnesota with enthusiasm I hadn't had a few hours before.

There were no long faces in the Minneapolis headquarters. Paul Sullivan had an astonishingly large crew, mainly volunteers, working the phones and planning schedules. Paul and his wife, Karen, live in Hawaii, but every four years they return to the Mainland to work for a Democratic candidate for president they believe in. They were admittedly "campaign junkies," and we were fortunate that they chose to help Paul Simon.

Many of our Iowa staff found their way to the Minneapolis office, still eager to help without any thought of pay. Paul Sullivan found homes for them to stay in, and saw that there was a supply of sandwich fixings and fruit. Although Governor Dukakis was running well in the polls, it was Paul Sullivan's impression that the Democrat Farm Labor spirit and the Hubert Humphrey legacy were more compatible and comfortable with the Paul Simon campaign. Bruce Babbitt withdrew from the race after New Hampshire. Gary Hart hung on.

Depending on the outcome of the Illinois primary on March 15, Paul would carry the campaign on to Michigan and Wisconsin. We were hoping for victory in Illinois, but not assuming anything at this perilous point in the campaign. We knew we had to do more campaigning in these states. Paul had been in Michigan several times, but it was now my turn to spend another day there. Students from Calvin College, a conservative school in Grand Rapids run by the Dutch Reform Church, gave me a hearty welcome. Elliott Jacobsen planned a solid day of interviews and receptions in Lansing and Flint. The crowds were large and supportive. I began to feel that we might have a chance here, although Dick Gephardt and Jesse Jackson were getting most of the attention from the press. When a tall, good-looking young man stepped up and said, "Hello, Aunt Jeanne," I was delighted to see my nephew, David Hurley, a student at Michigan State. His dad, my brother Bob, worked to get me elected to the Illinois General Assembly. David had organized student help for "Uncle Paul" and was an effective campaigner. State Representative Debbie Stabenow invited a group of women leaders to meet me. State Representative Dave Gubow and his wife packed their home and had a TV crew there as well.

Late that night at the Hilton Inn in Detroit, I decided not to let my expectations carry me too far away from harsh reality, and not kid myself. I was alone and tired and hadn't heard from Paul all day. I received confusing phone calls from Patty and Lea. One had me going to Rapid City or Sioux Falls in South Dakota and the other told me to go to Minneapolis for a reunion with Paul. While they tried to figure out a final schedule, I reached a low point.

I went to Sioux Falls, where Pam Huey and her parents, Sioux Falls residents, were doing all they could to muster a few votes for Paul with very little resources. Chris Sautter, Pam, her husband, Paul, and a few brave souls from Iowa, worked at the Simon headquarters. It was a valiant effort but Dick Gephardt swept South Dakota, and Paul ran third in Minnesota after Dukakis and Jesse Jackson. Student rallies at Gustavus Adolphus, a college in southern Minnesota, and the University of Minnesota, could not have gone better, but we were slipping and we knew it. Jesse Jackson's ability to attract crowds and the Dukakis organization and its money made a big difference. Gary Hart bowed out, coming in last in both states.

At a press conference on February 24, the day after the Minnesota and South Dakota contests, Paul acknowledged that he was behind, and that he would not spend money on TV or radio ads in the twenty southern states that made up Super

Tuesday. That was the equivalent of saying we had given up on winning any Southern delegates. Nevertheless, I continued with a trip to South Carolina.

In Greenville, I met a former school teacher of Jesse Jackson. She was justifiably proud of her student, who, she said, showed promise as a young man. At three events in Columbia, there was no press. But at St. Martin's Catholic Church, mainly a black parish, the pastor introduced me at the end of Mass, a rather unusual gesture that I appreciated.

But to add to our dismal picture, Paul told me that he had not done well in the Maine caucuses. We were trying to keep each other's morale up, but it wasn't working. I now began to worry about Paul's fate in the Illinois primary March 15.

Super Tuesday states on March 8 divided up among Governor Dukakis, Senator Gore, and Jesse Jackson. Dick Gephardt did not do well, taking only his home state of Missouri. Paul managed to pick up a handful of delegates. Although Governor Dukakis was leading in delegates, political pundits wrote columns and stories predicting no clear front-runner would emerge for a while, perhaps not until the convention. Although this analysis later proved faulty, it served to inspire us to make an all-out effort to capture Illinois delegates.

We faced several problems in Illinois. There were two "favorite sons"—Jackson and Simon. Our Illinois staff resisted any offers of help from the Iowa staff, claiming that they knew Illinois better. Paul declared that we would not spend a dime on any television or radio advertising. On top of all those factors, the *Chicago Sun-Times* and the *Chicago Tribune* polls did not look good. But, a campaign that appeared totally unorganized and chaotic at first, somehow quickly took shape. I agreed with Paul that his thirty-two years of public service in Illinois said more for him than thirty-second commercials could, but I privately worried that Governor Dukakis's planned expenditure of $500,000 on television advertising could be persuasive.

After a two-day respite in Makanda, Paul and I found new strength simply to be in Illinois. The familiar counties of Southern Illinois, the ward and township organizations of the City of Chicago and Cook County were waiting for us, and we knew what to do.

Freezing weather and snow and ice slowed us down, but friends and volunteers everywhere kept us going. Lea and I had the good fortune to have an excellent driver and a large comfortable car, which never left the icy roads. I debated Missouri Lieutenant Governor Harriet Woods in Springfield, where more than half the audience stood up and cheered me. Although Paul and I had supported Harriet in her campaign for U.S. senator, she was now working for Dick Gephardt, her fellow Missourian.

At a rally in the Forty-third Ward in Chicago, I thanked the good Democrats for all their help to Paul in 1984, and I asked for the same help this time around. Alderman Bernie Hansen, Ward committeeman Jack Merlo, and State Senator Dawn Clark Netsch assured me that they would do even better.

On one cold, icy March afternoon, I experienced one of the best stops of the whole Illinois campaign, although in the strictest sense it was not a campaign stop. At Witt School, in Montgomery County, Mrs. Becky Benson and her fifth-grade students raised money to purchase a flag that had flown over the U.S. Capitol. Paul's Senate staff asked me to make the presentation. Waiting to greet me were not only the fifth-graders and Mrs. Benson, but the entire student body, kindergarten through eighth grade, and faculty. I assured them this was not a campaign stop but one of the pleasant duties of a Senator's wife. I spoke about the flag, its meaning to American citizens, and welcomed questions. A little boy in the front row raised his hand, stood up and said, "I like you." He was such a darling, little boy, I hugged him on the spot! In August, I received a letter from Mrs. Benson, who told me that each class was given a tree on Arbor Day and asked to attach a verse or inscription. The fifth grade came up with these lines: " A symbol of love and beauty—dedicated to Mrs. Paul Simon."

Illinois was a fierce battleground for all the candidates that were left—Dukakis, Gore, Jackson, Gephardt and Paul—because of its 173 delegates to the Democratic Convention. The press with Paul dogged him with stories of imminent failure in Illinois. Our Chicago papers endorsed Dukakis and Gore, and their polls continued to show Paul slipping. We planned a victory party and hoped there would be something to celebrate. By now, we should have been depressed, but the receptions that Paul received everywhere, and the attention I was getting told us a different story.

In 1968, when Paul was a candidate for lieutenant governor of Illinois, he was not paired on the ballot with Democratic Governor Sam Shapiro, but ran with him. The papers and polls predicted the governor would lose, and assumed that Paul would also. But at every meeting we went to, someone would say, "Can I vote for the Republican candidate for governor, and for Paul too?" They could and did, resulting in the first and only election in Illinois of a governor and a lieutenant governor of different parties. A new Constitution several years later paired the two candidates, the same as the president and vice president on the national ticket. That was our first statewide campaign. Our reading of the electorate then told us that we had a chance and the same thing was happening this time. The polls just might be wrong.

Perry and Sheila were traveling the "blue highways" alone with instructions from the campaign treasurer to seek out friends to stay with or find a budget motel each night. After an experience when a county chair directed them to a home but had given the prospective host only a ten-minute warning, and several seedy, cheap motels, they were ready for a change.

Their chance to have a little fun and help Paul came when the producer of ABC's "Good Morning America" invited Sheila to appear on the morning of March 15 with Jesse Jackson, Jr., Neil Bush, and Robin Dole. Sheila and Perry quickly arranged to vote absentee at the Jackson County Courthouse in Murphysboro, drove 120 miles to St. Louis, and were the guests of ABC for the flight to New York. By this time, Sheila was comfortable with TV cameras, and fully prepared to discuss any issue, and to enjoy the interview.

The Golden Tulip Barbizon Hotel in New York City looked like the palace at Versailles to Sheila and Perry. Their room had two balconies, a king-size bed, and a basket full of lovely things like shower caps, two kinds of soap, and shampoo. Neil Bush and Sheila were the only two guests in the studio with Morton Dean. Sheila answered the first question, "What really bugs you about your dad, Sheila?" She responded she wished Paul wouldn't cut his own hair, as he did on occasion, but she said she understood that it was only part of being a fiscal conservative. (I must add that Paul only cuts his hair when he is desperate, not all the time, and that I can't stand to see him do it either.) The other children of the three candidates praised their fathers, said they never did anything that "bugged" them, and Neil Bush added that he believed his father was "too compassionate!" Sheila told me later that she thought she blew the campaign for Paul and should have been more adulatory after she heard Neil's fulsome praise. Naturally, I thought she was the most refreshing and candid guest. And that's what I told her when she called after the program.

Paul and I voted at the fire station in Makanda. A crowd of TV cameras and reporters followed us to our home to record the ceremonial tree planting that we have every primary and election day. In past years, we planted cherry and apple trees, dogwood, weeping willows, tulip poplars, and white pines. This year, I selected two Red Haven peach trees that The Family Tree Nursery assured me would thrive. While Paul dug the holes, about twenty members of the press watched and joked.

Arriving in Chicago, we wanted to know if the turnout was heavy or light and what the exit polls were saying. The morning papers said this was the end for Paul and predicted a Jackson victory.

We had a family-only pizza dinner at the Executive House before the polls closed at 7 P.M., and we flipped around the TV channels for any scrap of information. When the three networks declared Paul the winner, we refused to believe the good news and waited to see the county returns and to hear from our volunteers around the state. When we were sure that Paul had won, we followed the Secret Service agents in a circuitous route to the ballroom of the Midland Hotel, where we finally had an opportunity to cheer for Paul and savor a long-overdue victory. One staff member reported walking past the Secret Service command post when Dan Rather was projecting Paul the winner and hearing the agents cheer!

The final tally gave Paul 44 percent of the vote, Jesse Jackson 31 percent, and Governor Dukakis 17 percent. After spending more than $500,000, Governor Dukakis failed to win a single delegate. Jesse Jackson called to congratulate Paul and Paul congratulated him on running a clean campaign. While Jesse won the delegates in the three congressional districts that are mainly black, he failed to attract any sizable white vote.

After all the dire predictions of disaster, the political writers were puzzled. There was still no clear-cut front-runner. Paul's come-from-behind victory confounded the pundits, and the race was on again—this time in Michigan, a caucus state. We were cheerful once more to know that Paul was a player, and had bounced back. The nomination should have been locked up in Illinois; now talk about a "brokered" convention started again. I loved the headline in the *Detroit Free Press:* "Bush and Simon Take Illinois."

Our friends and volunteers in Michigan were ready to go again after the good news from Illinois. With Paul in Detroit, we walked in a Hamtramck neighborhood and stopped at a bakery where the owner presented me with a bouquet of red roses and a box of pastry. I believe I appreciated the calorie-laden pastry more than the flowers!

The candidates' wives were special guests at a Detroit Democratic Women's luncheon. Kitty Dukakis and Jane Gephardt spoke before me. Kitty left before I went on, but Jane remained to hear me. Our family voted Jane Gephardt "Miss Congeniality" in the field of candidates' wives since she always remembered names, always asked about our children, and projected warmth without being phony. Barbara Levin, wife of Senator Carl Levin, awarded me an "A" for my talk to the Democratic women.

That evening, Paul and I worked the room at a large Democratic dinner attended by about 2,400 people. A thoughtful waiter covered our dishes at the head table so we could get a quick bite before Paul spoke. This time, he departed from his usual stump speech, and was more incisive, and made a good impression.

In an intensive effort to make up for lost time, we did a fly-around in a small plane, stopping at Marquette, Traverse City, Grand Rapids, and then back to Detroit. At each stop, our advance team got a crowd and media. My friends from Calvin College met Paul and told him how they had been working for him.

We were at a dinner in Green Bay, Wisconsin, when news of the Michigan caucus results came in. Jesse Jackson made a surprise first-place showing. It was equally surprising that Governor Dukakis had failed yet again to win a major industrial state. Our showing was dismal.

The Michigan caucus marked the end of Congressman Gephardt's campaign. He withdrew and filed for his Congressional seat in Missouri. Jesse Jackson's overwhelming Michigan victory put still another spin on the primary picture. There could now be a wide-open convention, or a first-ballot nomination of Jesse Jackson. What had seemed impossible only a few months ago happened in Michigan—Reverend Jackson carried a Northern state.

Senator Gore and Paul were still candidates in the Wisconsin primary, but our team expected it to be the last one for us—unless a miracle occurred. The Wisconsin campaign turned into a tight race between Jackson and Dukakis, with Jesse picking up more strength every day.

Another nephew of mine, Kevin Hurley, active with student Democrats at the University of Wisconsin-LaCrosse, Andrea Durkin, and I went to work to do what we could in Marshfield, Wisconsin Falls, Wausau, Stevens Point, and Eau Claire. A rental Ford Tempo gave out in Pigeon Falls, but we carried on in a Chevy Blazer. Kevin was an excellent driver in fog, rain, and ice. The Wisconsin press surprised me by being so agreeable. They came to us, asked how much time we had to give them, and waited if there were others ahead of them.

A former classmate from St. Scholastica Academy in Chicago met me at a radio station in Wisconsin Falls, carrying pictures from an old yearbook. We held a mini class reunion while I waited for an interview. Kevin had to return to classes, Andrea went back to our Washington office, and I joined Paul and Martin, the Secret Service agents, and a shrinking media group.

At a family reunion in Green Bay, Wisconsin, we candidly discussed what options we had, and agreed that if we didn't score an upset in Wisconsin (which didn't seem likely) we would all welcome a vacation in Florida or Puerto Rico. Indeed, we needed a vacation somewhere! The months of strenuous campaigning, both exciting and exhausting, had taken their toll on our energy and emotions. We looked back to Iowa, New Hampshire, South Dakota, Minnesota, and Illinois with no regrets, but a lot of "what ifs?" Paul asked Martin to check out two or three possible vacation sites.

Together we drove to Zion Lutheran Church in Zachow where Paul's father, Pastor Martin Simon, had been baptized, confirmed, and ordained. It was a media event, to be sure, but also a return to roots for Paul, who greeted aunts, uncles, and cousins. We visited his grandparents' home, and the site of his great grandparents' dairy farm. In the small cemetery next to the church, we checked out the gravestones with all the family names. At least, Paul should be the "favorite grandson" in Wisconsin.

On a Sunday before the Wisconsin primary, we traveled in a small plane to several events including a shopping center in Oshkosh, a senior dinner in Milwaukee, a bowling alley in

Madison, and at last, dinner for two for Paul and me at a German restaurant in Milwaukee, recommended by Ed Garvey. The weiner schnitzel and *Liebfraumilch* were perfect. Paul and I felt that we had done all we could in Wisconsin. We were fully aware that Jesse Jackson's great momentum, and Dukakis's solid organization and healthy treasury left Gore and Simon in the distance.

In the midst of the anxiety of the Wisconsin primary, Paul was obliged to honor a commitment to a debate on urban problems at Fordham University in New York, and a day of campaign stops en route there. I could not believe that he would draw such favorable crowds in Syracuse, Rochester, and Mineola. The New York organizers were not giving up easily!

Rush-hour traffic slowed our arrival for the debate that had only Paul, Al Gore, and Jackson as participants. Governor Dukakis cited scheduling problems as an excuse for his absence. The students had a great time cheering and yelling for all the candidates. An unusually intense person in the audience interrupted Paul by yelling that the candidates were not talking about AIDS while people were dying. Upsetting as this was, Paul calmly waited until he finished and continued his reply.

The uncertainty of our status must have been working on my subconscious. Unable to sleep, I admired the view of New York City from the fortieth floor of our penthouse apartment that Stanley Lewis so kindly allowed us to use when we were in New York, and I wondered what it would be like to be normal people again.

We decided our last days in Wisconsin should not be marked by lassitude or recriminations, and to relax a bit. With that attitude, Sheila, Perry, and I took off for scheduled stops at Fond Du Lac, Oshkosh, Sheboygan, Manitowoc, and Appleton. In Oshkosh, we located the "Oshkosh, B'Gosh" factory store and indulged ourselves by buying blue jeans and shirts. It was fun to laugh and talk with Sheila and Perry in between radio and newspaper interviews. On Good Friday, we gathered in

Wausau at the home of Uncle Hank, where Aunt Dee and cousin Lois Simon brought out old family pictures of Paul's Wisconsin relatives. Paul was relaxed and happy.

On a rainy Sunday before the Wisconsin primary, after several campaign stops, Paul typed a draft of his withdrawal statement. I read it with a heavy heart—good writing as always by Paul—but hard to read with tears in my eyes. We did our best at dinner that evening to be cheerful, recalling old family stories and past campaigns. We just wanted this one to end, and to get on with our lives.

Typical of Paul, our last campaign event was a visit to the unemployment office in Milwaukee, so he could assess the true dimensions of the country's unemployment for himself. He spoke at length with a black woman who had been out of work for six months. She was the sole support of her three children, had been laid off her job as a fork-lift operator and hoped for some job equal to her skills. Paul's genuine concern for the less fortunate was obvious. He requested a follow-up on her case from the person in charge of the office.

After a long walk back to our hotel and trailed by camera crews and reporters looking for the last word from the next candidate about to leave the fray, we packed up and headed for Washington to wait for the expected results.

My journal ended there with these words—"Our mood is still generally cheerful; Paul is an eternal optimist."

★ 12 ★

Return to Normal Life

The strong victory for Governor Dukakis in Wisconsin prolonged the primary season. New York became the next focus of attention with its April 19 primary. Paul announced he would hold a press conference on April 7 at which, the media assumed, he would withdraw from the list of presidential contenders.

The Secret Service agents for "Scarlett" left before Paul made his way through a huge crowd to a hearing room in the Dirksen Senate Office Building. I steeled myself not to cry and I didn't, but I noticed some young campaign staff men and women with moist eyes, as they listened to Paul give his farewell address.

> I am today suspending my campaign for the presidency. I'm grateful to all who have campaigned with me and for me. And I leave the field of active campaigning with no regrets for having made the race.

He left the campaign as he had entered it a year earlier—with class, and with a challenge to Americans to continue to strive to do better, "to form a more perfect union," in the words of the U.S. Constitution.

Our choice for a vacation settled on Palmas del Mar in Puerto Rico. Martin made reservations for our departure immediately after Paul's press conference. An hour later it was "wheels up" for Puerto Rico where a week of sunshine, swimming, fishing, and tennis restored our morale and vitality.

With surprising ease, Paul and I, Martin, Sheila, and Perry returned to being "ordinary people," no longer intensely preoccupied with the hard task of campaigning every day. It was good to be in control of our lives, without a schedule telling us where to go, whom to meet, and what to say. Paul returned to the Senate, a better senator for the experience he gained in a nationwide campaign.

The business of settling accounts, disposing of furniture and equipment, and providing information that the Federal Elections Committee requires continued long after the campaign was suspended. We also had a sizable debt to vendors and staff, which required immediate attention.

While I wanted as much as possible to put the primaries and caucuses behind me, and not to dwell on what might have been, some disturbing factors about the Iowa caucuses returned to haunt us. On May 15, the NBC Nightly News featured a discussion of the confusing results of the Iowa caucuses. NBC reporter Tom Pettit interviewed a group of Iowans and Hugh Winebrenner, a Drake University political science professor, who said that if all the votes had been counted on the night of February 8, it was possible that Paul Simon might have won the popular vote. Bonnie Campbell, the chair of the Iowa Democratic Party, agreed it was certainly possible that Simon could have won, and that she did not know what the final tally was! It seemed incredible to me that the head of the Iowa Democratic Party would make such an admission.

An article in the June 1988 issue of *American Politics* by William Saletan enlarged further on this theme. In "The Phantom Poll Booth" he concluded that systematic problems "rendered the National Election Service figures absolutely worthless as a final authority on the caucus outcome." Since ABC and CBS reported Gephardt the winner based on NES figures, he added, "maybe Paul Simon wasn't really the loser he was reported to be." NBC waited twenty-four hours and then showed

Gephardt leading by only a half-point margin, though they said it was too close to call.

For all the students, the volunteers, the bow-tie brigades from Illinois, and all the people who worked for Paul in Iowa who believed that the Iowa Democratic Party conducted the caucuses in a fair and honest fashion, this was depressing news. I was not only depressed, I was angry at the party officials who had allowed it to happen.

The New York primary ended all doubt as to who the Democratic nominee would be—Governor Dukakis was a clear winner. There remained only the Democratic Convention in July to confirm the nomination by the delegates. I had no desire to go to the convention, and would have been more than happy to watch it on television, but Paul convinced me that it would be worthwhile, and that he didn't want to go alone. He was right, as usual. Delegates from across the United States recognized and congratulated Paul on his efforts to win the nomination.

We met people who had helped us in Iowa, New Hampshire, Minnesota, South Dakota, and those who wanted to vote for Paul in other states. With the exception of the Jackson delegates, the Illinois delegates remained firm for Paul, but cast their votes for Governor Dukakis in the end. At a reception we held for supporters, Paul and I had an opportunity to thank everyone who had been with us. As Paul made the rounds of television and radio interviews, he was stopped repeatedly by people who wanted his autograph, or to have their picture taken with him. I even managed to greet Bonnie Campbell with a degree of cordiality that surprised me.

The mood of the convention was one of reconciliation, and I went along with that spirit. On the final night as Paul and I joined the winners and losers on the stage after Governor Dukakis's acceptance speech, I could only think that we were fortunate to have participated in the process that allows Americans to select a leader every four years. Wearing the green linen dress Sheila made for me, I linked arms with Paul and sang "God Bless America" with all the feeling I could muster. On that evening I happily contemplated a Democratic victory in November.

Paul and I pledged to Governor Dukakis and to Senator Bentsen that we would campaign for them or with them wherever we were needed. For Paul, that meant more travel and speeches in California, New York, Pennsylvania, Ohio, Oregon, Washington State, Minnesota, New Jersey, and Illinois. I worked with the Dukakis campaign in Illinois and helped local candidates for the Legislature and Congress. Late in October, North Shore Congregation Israel in Glencoe, Illinois, held a candidates' forum for Kitty Dukakis. Anne Roosevelt, a granddaugther of Eleanor Roosevelt, asked me to introduce Kitty. Thirty-two years ago I spoke to the North Shore Congregation Israel and asked them for their help in my first legislative race. This night, I asked them for their help for Governor Dukakis. Up until Election Day, the presidential race in Illinois was too close to call. We continued to hope that Illinois would carry for Governor Dukakis.

A few hours after the polls closed, we prematurely celebrated a victory for Governor Dukakis when the networks projected him a winner in Illinois. The projections were wrong and we admitted defeat around midnight. It was over. The Democrats nationally lost for the third straight time. A year of our lives seeking the nomination and then working for a Democratic victory had been almost in vain. We lost the presidency, though I hope the ideals and dreams and programs we talked about will live on.

Would the end result have been different if Paul were the candidate? I don't know, but I believe Paul would have spelled out a vision for America with warmth and conviction. I know he would have defined "liberal" in ways that working men and women would not object to. Social Security, Medicare, college loans, equal educational opportunities were all liberal programs when they began. The qualities that the *Des Moines Register* noted in its endorsement of Paul would hold up well in debates with the Republican candidate. He never would have allowed negative advertising that demeaned him or his patriotism to pass unnoticed.

In an election characterized by thirty-second sound bites, negative advertising, little or no discussion of national issues, abbreviated debates, and media more interested in the "horse race" than in the candidates' position on issues, Paul could have risen above the pettiness and attracted a broad spectrum of people concerned about the quality of life for their children and grandchildren.

The question I am most often asked is, "Would you do it again?" I have to admit I don't want to repeat that experience. But if anyone asks if I regret taking a year to campaign and then lose, I can honestly say I have no regrets. Tough and demanding as it was to be on the hustings, it was also the experience of a lifetime that very few people are privileged to have.

Our lives, and those of our children, were enriched by working for Paul's nomination. We worked as a team for a goal that turned out to be unobtainable, but we gained a knowledge of the needs of Americans that we will never forget.

While shopping at a Washington supermarket recently, I was surprised when a young man said, "Aren't you Mrs. Simon?" And then he told me that he and his wife, both lawyers, admired my role in the campaign and voted for Paul because they thought we were a good team for the White House and the country. I thanked him on behalf of the Simon and Simon team.